ANTIQUE
BLUE and
WHITE
SPODE

263117
738.2 | WILLIAMS | Antique Blue & White Spode

10.2

Hertfordshire
COUNTY COUNCIL
Community Information

- 4 JUN 2003

Please renew/return this item by the last date shown.

So that your telephone call is charged at local rate, please call the numbers as set out below:

	From Area codes 01923 or 020:	From the rest of Herts:
Renewals:	01923 471373	01438 737373
Enquiries:	01923 471333	01438 737333
Minicom:	01923 471599	01438 737599

L32　　　　　　www.hertsdirect.org

Fig. 1 Spode Soup Plate " Chase after a Wolf "

ANTIQUE
BLUE and WHITE
SPODE

By

SYDNEY B. WILLIAMS

With a Foreword by

H. GRANVILLE FELL
Editor of *The Connoisseur*

WITH 123 ILLUSTRATIONS

B. T. BATSFORD LTD.
15 NORTH AUDLEY STREET, LONDON, W.1
& MALVERN WELLS, WORCESTERSHIRE

First Edition published Winter, 1943.

*Made and Printed in Great Britain
at the Chaseton Press, London, W.C.1.*

DEDICATED

BY GRACIOUS PERMISSION

TO

HER MAJESTY QUEEN MARY

ACKNOWLEDGMENT

To A. Gresham Copeland, Esq., is due an expression of appreciation for his encouragement in the writing of this book and constant help throughout with detailed information culled from his vast knowledge of potting and of Spode's early manufactures, also for the loan of many copperplate prints from the originals still in the possession of the Spode Works of Messrs. W. T. Copeland and Sons, Ltd., which are included in this book, and without which the record would be incomplete.

In addition, I have to thank Mr. Copeland for his infinite patience and trouble in replying to my constant demands for information, and while he is in no sense responsible for any expression of opinion, appreciation, or of criticism, either adverse or favourable, it would indicate a lack of gratitude if his assistance were not acknowledged.

S. B. W.

WAR may destroy in a few months what craftsmen have taken centuries to produce, but it cannot kill the desire to look at beautiful things, nor the pleasure of using and possessing them. On the contrary, as these things become rarer under the ravages of war, there awaken in people a new appreciation of the heritage they are losing and an anxiety to preserve it.

Every piece that is acquired then becomes a treasure to possess and an incitement to find more. The careful and conscientious collector is thus a guardian of his country's culture.

There are many valuable things to which a collector may give his attention. Among them an honourable place must be given to the products of our early potters. It is the writer's hope that the following record will play some small part in assisting the preservation and protection of our national inheritance.

CONTENTS

Contents

LIST OF ILLUSTRATIONS

XIII

List of Illustrations

List of Illustrations

List of Illustrations

Foreword

" Antiquity !   Thou wondrous charm, what art thou ?
That being nothing, art everything " asks Charles Lamb.
" What mystery lurks in this retroversion ? "   All lovers of
bygone things can give the answer.   Antiquity inspires rever-
ence.   It is as potent a spell as ancestor worship is to the
Chinese.   But why should we collect so comparatively recent
a thing as Spode ?   Partly because of its intrinsic excellence
and beauty, and partly because it is a field as yet not over-
worked.   New things become old and take their turn and each
succeeding generation brings its own contingent of collectors.
And so the wares of Spode honoured in more than a century
and a half of birthdays have joined the goodly company of
' Antiques.'   Spode is neither too rare, nor too plentiful to
put the would-be collector off, neither is it necessarily expensive,
but like other desirable things, must be sought with patience
and discrimination.

The author of this book has been a discerning collector
for many years.   So well informed is he on his subject that his
pages may be taken as a standard guide for those who would
follow in his footsteps.   He is the Columbus who has charted
their new world.   The enthusiasm he displays is well-found,
being based on practical knowledge, the result of long familiarity
with the products of the early English potters and especially
with those of his particular choice.   This enthusiasm he is

happy to share with others and so, in his unselfishness (a quality somewhat rare in hunters of antiques) he blazes the trail for those who would share his favourite sport. His clues and descriptions of the many and various patterns, with their prototypes, including a number of as yet undiscovered examples, will increase the reader's interest and enhance the ardour of the chase.

Naturally it will be asked ' Where are these happy hunting grounds ? ' Even these are indicated. Safety may be found in the experienced hands of reputable dealers, and especially in those of the British Antique Dealers' Association, whose avowed aim it is to serve its patrons faithfully. The author mentions the Caledonian Market, a universal caravanserai of all kinds of commodities, as a possible cover for this species of quarry. Anything might be found there. Junk shops need not be overlooked. Readers might also search among the homes of their older relatives for forgotten crocks at the backs of cupboards. The family kitchen dresser comes to mind, which but a few years back was piled with the remains of a fine service, never used because incomplete and ' old fashioned,' and now alas, beyond recall.

I expect that, after a perusal of this book, many a roving eye will be directed to antique shops, old store cupboards, attics and country auction rooms, and I can say nothing better in favour of it than that Mr. Williams has made me like Spode myself—only, I recommend his readers to do their seeking with dispatch.

H. GRANVILLE FELL.

Introduction

THIS book is written by a Collector for Collectors. Some people say Collectors do not now exist, that a car and a gallon of " gas " is the beginning and end of the requirements of the people of this generation ; that this is a machine age and only machines are of interest.

This materialistic outlook should not deter a possible Collector, for have there not been Collectors of the antique and the beautiful since the days that History was recorded ?

" The beautiful " is a description that can truly be applied to the work of the Potter who, with his hands and the common earthly clay, has fashioned many works of art for the eye to behold and even the poor to possess.

In addition to the Collector, this book it is felt will appeal to all lovers of beautiful things ; to those appreciative of the arts of a past generation, and to those who delight in turning back to a page of history not so far remote as to be beyond the thrill which comes to us as we hear about the comings and goings of our own grandparents or great-grandparents.

In dealing with the subject of Blue and White SPODE ware, it is the wish of the writer to emphasize the beauty of and increase interest in these articles which were originally made for utility and are now prized as antiques and acknowledged as an accepted amenity in the life of today.

The Rt. Hon. Winston Churchill, M.P., wrote recently : " We come somewhat abruptly to the modern age. It began at the very earliest one hundred years ago. Man had been

1

groping and fumbling for science and machinery. In the Nineteenth Century he got them into his hands. Every year saw great leaps forward. Tremendous discoveries were made about the physical universe around us. Mighty powers were harnessed to the service of our material needs."

Josiah Spode the first was born before those 100 years began, in the Eighteenth Century (1733) and died shortly before the century's close (1797).

His son, Josiah Spode the second, also the maker of the Blue and White ware reviewed in this work, was born at Stoke-on-Trent in 1754, when his father was twenty-one years of age.

Josiah Spode, the father, was apprenticed at the age of sixteen to Thomas Whieldon, one of the most fertile and inventive potters of his day, on the 9th November, 1749. In 1754 he left Whieldon and at Stoke-on-Trent began in a small way to manufacture Blue and White ware and coloured pottery.

Eight years later we find him managing works at Stoke for William Banks, and in the same year, 1762, he was engaged as a master potter in his own name up to the year 1776, when, as it is recorded, he purchased these pot works at Stoke.

It was at these works that the son received his training as a potter and of which he eventually became the owner. The works still operate on the same spot at the present day and are known as the Spode Pottery.

In 1779 the father took into partnership William Copeland and the son went to London to assist him at the new warehouse opened in Lincoln's Inn Fields.

From these dates it can be assumed that the son had spent those nine years learning the business of a potter and now was to learn the business of a salesman of a product of which he knew more than an average workman.

Reviewers of the Spodes have never drawn any special attention to William Copeland who was said to be a native

Fig. 2   Original engraving of Coaches leaving London for Northern
Cities.   Published 1825.

of Stoke-on-Trent, formerly in the tea trade. It was to assist him in this trade that he proposed to sell the products—cups and saucers—of Josiah Spode. Modern businesses realise the immense importance of the sales side, and William Copeland must have been one of those Sales Managers whose able efforts were a very decided factor in promoting the success of the Spode works.

It should be recorded that during this period, according to Simeon Shaw (History of the Staffordshire Potteries, 1829), " In one year the clear profits of the London business alone exceeded £13,000."

If Josiah Spode the first was a good potter, then William Copeland was equally a good salesman, and Josiah Spode the son had the good fortune to learn both sides of his business from two experts. Thus, as we review the Blue and White manufactured by the son, we realise he inherited a legacy of learning and example from these two men which he put to good use.

In 1797 Josiah Spode the first died and his son returned to Stoke and took over the business of a potter, continuing until his death in 1827.

CHAPTER I

The History of the Period

TO present, with success, the history of the first quarter of the Nineteenth Century in a single chapter would be impossible.

I shall attempt no more, therefore, than to remind the reader of some salient facts which may, in a measure, form a useful background when considering the creative period of Spode's time.

The first important fact relates to the population of the British Isles. Looking back to the early part of the Eighteenth Century, we find that the manufacture of cotton was largely the cause of the improved health, progress and prosperity which prevailed during the time Spode was in business.

Previous to this cotton manufacture the people were clothed in poor fabrics which were worn until they fell to pieces. With the introduction of cotton goods, the poor were able to buy cheap clothes ; in fact, underclothes, first introduced in the Eighteenth Century, were only made possible by this cheap cotton.

Of more significance was the consequent increase in hygiene. Cotton garments were easily washed, and because of this new cleanliness, better health resulted, the death rate was reduced and infant mortality with it. A considerable increase in the population resulted, thus creating a bigger market for all manufacturers.

This bigger market, therefore, and its influence on domestic life is our first salient fact.

The political history of this time was equally remarkable. The rule of the great Napoleon Bonaparte began in the latter part of the Eighteenth Century, reached its zenith about 1805, and terminated in 1815 (Battle of Waterloo, June, 1815).

To be a manufacturer when the threat of invasion was ever present was the lot of Josiah Spode, who, because of this danger, was gazetted as Captain of the Staffordshire Yeomanry, Pottery Troop, in 1798 (*London Gazette*, July 7th, 1798), and continued to hold this appointment until October, 1805.

The Battle of Trafalgar which took place on October 21st, 1805, shattered the power of France and Spain at sea at a time when Napoleon had made himself master of Europe.

Nelson's victory saved England from all chance of invasion and gave to all manufacturers of the country freedom to work without hindrance.

Thus, in a few words, we have the second salient fact.

The third outstanding characteristic of this first quarter of the Nineteenth Century (roughly designated as the Regency Period) was the standard of craftsmanship.

It is difficult to realise that no manufacturing machinery existed with the probable exception of a steam engine provided with leather belts connected to the crushing mills. The potter's wheel, possibly the lathe, was driven by man's own foot-power and later may have been driven by belts from the steam engine. These simple machines had little in common with the machines of our own day.

Hence all the goods of this period are almost entirely hand-made and reveal originality of design and the quality of the craftsman's workmanship.

There are, however, some very interesting side issues that may be considered, and which were due to the lack of more recent conveniences.

Perhaps the first to come to mind is the absence of steam traction. No passenger trains were in existence and ordinary

travellers used the Stage Coach (Figure 2). It is interesting
to recall that these stage coaches were well organised, ran to
schedule, and travelled up and down the country by day and
all through the night, in a well ordered manner, thanks to
McAdam and Telford, who were the pioneers of our road
making. The first of these two men left a legacy in the
substance now universally known as " macadam," which is
used for the surfacing of our roads. It should be noted, too,
that the traveller of these days was much troubled by the clouds
of dust, which the four horses and the coach made in their
progress along the country roads. The pedestrian and farmer
added their complaints to those of the traveller as this white
powder settled upon their persons and lands and spoiled the
countryside. In the rainy season the mud was perhaps an
even a greater trouble.

We may remember, too, that all this now antique pottery
must have travelled many miles along these roads, in market
carts, to its various destinations in the cities of our land ;
yet much of it still remains whole for our pleasure, a fact
which seems little short of miraculous !

The absence of the camera for the making of pictures
is the second side issue which is significant. If a picture were
required, the only way to obtain it was to sit down quietly
and make a drawing. Should this method be not sufficiently
enlightening, then a water-colour or an oil painting would be
the only possible alternative for securing the desired effect.
When more than one copy was required, the only known
method of duplicating the picture was by means of the
engraved copperplate or the wood-cut.

The potter had become a producer of pictures in a world
considerably lacking at that time in these ornaments.

The absence of recreation, as we know it today, is the
next significant fact which had its effect upon the making of
pottery.

Imagine no cinemas, very few theatres, no football matches, no holidays (Christmas and Good Friday only), no Saturday afternoon holiday, and although horse-racing was becoming popular, it had not yet reached the citizen.

The coffee house, gaming club and private entertaining were the diversions of the monied class.

Thus the potter was provided with a market for his wares which was reflected in the sumptuously loaded tables and decorations of many fancy shaped dishes used for these entertainments. London people ate hot suppers, besides a substantial dinner in the middle of the day. Many ate and drank too much and it is true to say of those days that the table killed more than the sword.

Gambling and card playing were in vogue and the potter provided the supper dishes for serving refreshment on such occasions—four semi-circular dishes, with covers, and a centre dish, all in the compass of a mahogany tray.

Families were large and dinner services were in proportion. Many of these old services which have survived consist of nearly 200 pieces.

The Blue and White ware made by Spode was not purchased by the poor. It was intended to appeal to the professional man, the doctor and lawyer and to the wealthy merchant. Well-to-do business men delighted in entertaining their friends ; these were the chief customers for this product of the potteries—not only in this country but also on the Continent, where English goods were bought for the adornment of the house and the service of the table.

CHAPTER II

Blue and White

JOSIAH SPODE, the second, produced the best Blue and White ware of his time. This is a statement that may well be challenged, and therefore needs to be made good.

It was first made by Simeon Shaw (*History of the Staffordshire Potteries, 1829*). Following Shaw, Chaffers comments that Spode was " the most successful manufacture of his time and acquired a large fortune in business."

Jewitt remarks that the porcelain, the ironstone china and the ordinary earthenware manufactures at this time were of the very highest character, in body, in glaze and in decoration ; indeed in all three respects they rank with the best of the period.

J. F. Blacker, a more modern writer (*The A B C of Nineteenth-Century English Ceramic Art*) states : " I believe that the potters and writers on pottery have scarcely done justice to Josiah Spode the second. If any one man is responsible for the concentrated china-making in the Staffordshire Potteries he is that man, for he it was who raised the art to its highest level of practical utility, and more than that, his finest productions compare, and not unfavourably, with the best that other factories have made."

In the long run, the best evidence of the truth of the contention is contained in the articles themselves.

10

Close examination shows that the potting was very good, the various shapes and details, such as handles, reveal a careful designing and modelling ; small articles such as the Tea strainer and Mustard pot, provide examples of thoughtful designing. The plates and dishes, covers and stands, all reveal the same care in designing and modelling.

With regard to the illustrations, it is impossible to claim that these were entirely original in conception. The well known and important Willow pattern, the forerunner of these blue and white all-over patterns, had set the course for every potter to follow.

There appears to be a gap between the production of this first design and the introduction of the many new designs which followed. Spode was one of the first, if not actually the first, to bring new ideas into the field.

Jewitt in 1883 is the only writer who has given us a full list, with dates, of these productions ; where he obtained his information cannot be ascertained, and even the names of the patterns are impossible to identify with certainty.

The most interesting of Spode's patterns, the Indian Sporting Series, may be considered as entirely original in their use as designs for table ware. Other designs appear to have been equally original as regards the selection of subjects, though the idea of using existing engravings for adaptation to table ware decoration was no longer new. The actual craftsmanship, designing, proportion and all practical details, in the aggregate, form entirely original productions and reflect great credit on Spode. This was a worthy contribution to English pottery of this class.

The printing of the pictures reveals an equal excellence. Borders do not run over the edges and the joinings are difficult to perceive (this in contrast to the wares of other manu-facturers) ; the pictures are very clear ; there is no smudging caused by carelessness in the transferring, and the colour of the blue in many cases approaches the best blue colour of the Chinese K'ang Hsi porcelain.

The blue colour, as in the Chinese, varies.   Some specimens are faint in colour, others deeper, but taken as a class the blue is particularly attractive and has come to be known as " Spode Blue " in references to the ware of this period.

The body, too, varies in colour, in the majority of specimens being remarkable for its pure whiteness, while some are more cream in colour.   The light weight of individual plates and dishes is noticeable when compared with modern counterparts, and must be accounted for by the absence of modern machinery.

The glaze is silky and soft to the touch, with a smoothness and absence of bubble, remarkable for ware made when the industry was still in its early stages.

This is the evidence which is produced to support the statement that Spode made " the best blue and white ware of his time."

CHAPTER III

Dates of Manufacture

IT is natural that the possessor of an antique object of art should desire to know the exact date of the manufacture of his particular specimen. It is easy to date Spode's Blue and White to a general period from 1781 to 1833, but to state with absolute accuracy the particular year that any given pattern was produced is an impossible task.

The question of the dates of production of the wares of the early English Potters has been dealt with by several writers. William Turner, in his *Transfer Printing on Enamels, Porcelain and Pottery, 1907*, has reviewed the subject of printed ware very carefully, but he refrains from giving exact dates, preferring to classify his sections as Eighteenth Century, late Eighteenth Century and early Nineteenth Century. In spite of his care in allocation, he has erroneously included in the Eighteenth Century class Spode's Indian Sporting Design. In justice to William Turner, however, it must be noted that in his " Remarks " column he gives the date of the factory : Circa 1784-1833.

A careful perusal of his book reveals the fact that most of the engravers' work in the Eighteenth Century was used in the production of black transfer work *over* the glaze, the *underglaze* blue transfer work consisting mainly of reproductions of the " Willow " and its variants, adapted by the potters of that time. The acceptance by the public of this newer form of decoration with its better wearing qualities, would suggest that the demand created for this particular pattern made the introduction of new patterns unnecessary, and that the market had not yet come to saturation point. It appears that the need for new patterns was not reached until about 1805 and again, that Spode was one of the first if not the first, to provide these new patterns.

Another writer has reviewed the work of Spode in greater detail. L. Jewitt (*The Ceramic Art of Great Britain, 1883*) provides us with a list of Titles and the dates of their introduction.

Castle	1806	Panel Japan	1820
Roman	1812	Geranium	,,
Turk	1813	Oriental	,,
Milkmaid	1814	Font	1821
Dagger Border	,,	Marble	,,
Tower	,,	Bud & Flower	1822
Peacock	,,	Sun	,,
New Temple	,,	Bonpot	,,
New Nankin	1815	Union	,,
New Japan	,,	Double Bonpot	1823
India	,,	Blue Border	,,
Italian	1816	Filigree	,,
Woodman	,,	Image	1824
Blossom	1817	Persian	,,
Pale Broseley	,,	Etruscan	1825
Waterloo	1818	Bamboo	,,
Arcade	,,	Blue Imperial	1826
Lucano	1819	Union Wreath	,,
Ship	,,		

Many of these titles have been identified. The dates of their introduction pose a more difficult problem. No confirmation can be obtained at the Spode Works with regard to Jewitt's dates and the only evidence obtainable has been the dates of publication of engravings which inspired the different designs.

If the " Roman " 1812 referred to is the " Tiber " pattern, then the date may be approximately correct, as the aquatint from which the design was taken was published in 1798.

The " Turk " design of 1813 is the Caramanian described herein. The date is approximately correct, but as the " Indian Sporting " designs must have preceded the " Caramanian ; the reference to " India " 1815 must be considered to be inaccurate if the " Sporting " design is meant. (There is a pattern called " India " which is entirely different from " Indian Sporting.") The two patterns, Indian Sporting and Caramanian will always be of the greatest interest to collectors because of their outstanding originality, and also because of the many different pictures which went to make these two dinner services, in contrast to the single illustration which in other cases forms the basis of the pattern.

Too much reliance must not be placed upon the dates given by Jewitt. His first date of 1806 may not be early enough. He maintains that one only of the Italian pictures was produced at that date, although four pictures were produced by Spode from the same series of engravings. According to Jewitt a lapse of thirteen years occurs before Spode produced the last design of the series. Here again we may dispute this Author's conclusions. It would be reasonable to assume that the Italian designs, " Castle," " Roman," " Tower," " Lucano," followed each other in a sequence. In the absence of any evidence, the facts of the case remain a matter for conjecture.

The subject of the dates of the Blue and White designs is frequently debated and the collector of Spode ware will find it difficult to allocate specimens which were made between the years 1781/1784 (when Spode the first is said to have introduced underglaze printing) and the year 1806 mentioned by Jewitt as the date of the introduction of the Castle pattern.

We may assume that the " Willow " pattern, in its various

forms, was the chief motive of the Blue and White designs at that time and also that underglaze printing was being used in producing many patterns of the porcelain wares.

We have to remember that " Stone China " was introduced in 1805 and we know that many of the Anglo-Chinese patterns of the famille-rose type were produced upon this ware, the outline designs of some patterns being produced by the use of the blue underglaze printing.

It is certain that the prototype engravings used were dated 1796/1798 (Castle, Roman, Tower, Lucano) 1803 (Caramanian) and 1805/1807 (Indian Sporting). It is not possible, however, to give exact dates to any of the Chinese prototypes used by Spode, but we do know that they were earlier than the engravings.

No one looking at this list of Jewitt's titles, which he describes as " some " of Spode's productions, could state that Spode was lacking in originality. Moreover, it must be remembered that every different subject had to have a border specially designed to be in harmony, a task in which originality and artistry were conspicuously successful. This list does not take into account the output of porcelain productions which was taking place at the same time.

The experienced collector finds no difficulty in identifying the manufactures of Spode without the aid of the marking on the reverse of his specimens, but a new collector may justly be puzzled when it is found that some patterns introduced by Spode are marked " Copeland & Garrett " or " Copeland & Sons." His bewilderment serves to demonstrate the success of these patterns, for the markings show that they have been in continuous production, in some cases to the present date. Many of Spode's productions were unmarked and can only be recognised today by those who have become accustomed to the handling of these early productions.

CHAPTER IV

Engravings

A NEW movement came at the end of the eighteenth century—the portrayal of the famous sages and heroes of antiquity.

This is revealed in the engravings of the period, and as the movement spread it came to the potter to add his own contribution.

The inscriptions used by the engravers are not familiar in these days, and are therefore given here with their meanings.

Sometimes the painter engraved his own picture and this work is denoted by the term *pinxit*, which is, literally, " painted it."

More often the work of engraving was carried out by another artist, a specialist in one or more of the several forms of engraving and the different materials employed. The term *sculpsit*, "engraved it," would then follow the name of this artist-engraver.

Another Latin word, *delineavit*, or its abbreviation, denotes the man who " drew it," thus distinguishing between an engraving taken from a painting and one taken from a drawing. After the artist's name the word *fecit*, " he made it " is usual.

The order of introduction of the various styles of engraving were, line, etching, mezzotint, stipple and aquatint.

Spode used as models aquatints of his period and as this is seldom used now a few words regarding these engravings will be apposite.

The use of *aqua fortis* in eating or biting away the metal gave the name to the process of aquatinting. Therefore, prints made by the assistance of acids were an early instance of the application of chemicals for simplifying manufacture.

By covering the copper plate with resin, which the acid could not penetrate, the surface was prepared for the design. Upon this the acid was allowed to do its work in successive bitings.

When a copper plate was immersed in the acid, the acid would eat into the metal without variation, and therefore the process had to be executed by degrees. Portions requiring greater depth would require longer immersion and light portions much less. Hence a process of " stopping out " had to be employed, in order to obtain the correct result. It was a slow and difficult process yet yielded beautiful results,

Aquatinting was not finished with the making of the copper plate. Equally difficult was the printing that followed. In the case of a colour aquatint the different coloured inks used had to be applied to the plate by hand, and each confined to the portion designed to take it. The whole of the plate could not be inked at one process as in a mono-chrome. The final print of such an aquatint resembled a water-colour painting, printed in colours. Further colours were frequently added by hand, after the initial colour prints had been made.

Many aquatints were entirely coloured by hand, in fact

the tinting of aquatints was quite a considerable industry. When colour-printing was actually applied to aquatints, very often no more than two tints were used.

From the method of copper plate printing, in which the plate is placed, after inking, under pressure with the dampened paper on its face to receive the impression, we also get the term " plate mark." The copper plate, being smaller than the paper, would leave its indent visible round the edges, and when the paper was dry, this marking remained.

The Potter's method of printing was somewhat similar to that of the ordinary printer, but he produced his copper plate by engraving and not etching, and it had to be more deeply cut than for printing on paper.

The copper plate is engraved exactly as it would appear on the ware. This copper plate, which is about an eighth of an inch thick, is placed over a stove to be heated. Then the colour which has been mixed into a stiff paste in oil, is worked into the channels of the plate which constitute the design. All superfluous colour is then wiped off and the surface of the copper plate, being free from colour substance, will not print but forms the white portions of the print. A sheet of prepared tissue-paper made wet with a solution of soap and water is carefully laid, without any wrinkles, on the surface of the copper plate, and then both are passed through the rollers of a press. The copperplate is next placed on the stove to be sufficiently heated to enable the tissue-paper to be peeled off. The transfer is now ready, with its sticky surface bearing the engraved pattern upon it, to be applied to the white body of the ware, which is in the biscuit state, that is to say without any glaze upon it. By the skilful use of scissors all superfluous paper is cut away and the design is applied or transferred to the ware. Care is necessary to ensure that the joins in the pattern are neatly and accurately made and that the sticky printing remains untouched by the fingers. The back of the tissue, through which the design can be clearly seen, is rubbed with a ball pad and lubricated with soap. The ware is next immersed in a tub of water, and the tissue paper floats off, leaving the oil-printed design upon the ware ready for the next operation of dipping in the glaze. Finally it is passed into the glost oven.

The art of producing pictures by means of engraving had reached an advanced stage by the time that Spode made use of them as models. Aquatints were at the height of their popularity. Many were being printed in colours, and many others were having the colours added by hand after the initial printing in a single or two colours.

The potter had tried his hand with colours but with the exception of the blue colour, he came up against many difficulties. When placed in the oven the colours lost their original value, being affected by the great heat necessary for glazing. It was therefore necessary to add these colours *after* the glaze had been applied—or to " over-glaze " them—and then fire them at a lower temperature so as not to spoil the colour values.

Other colours than the blue had been used for underglaze printing but the success not being so sure, it can be said that little was attempted in a commercial way at this period.

The Indian Sporting Scenes from the book " Oriental Field Sports " were from sketches by the author, Captain Thomas Williamson, suitably worked up for reproduction as aquatints by Samuel Howitt (sometimes spelled Howett), an artist well known for his drawings of animals.

A third artist, sometimes more than one, was employed to etch the pictures on the copper plate.

Thus we find engraved on the picture : " Saml. Howett, del., from the original design of Captn. Thos. Williamson. H. Merke, Sculp."

The aquatints are known as Samuel Howitt's work, but are sometimes described as " after Howitt," because he did not actually etch the copper plate.

The use of engravings as subjects for the potters' art was not a new idea. All the potters of this country and also those on the Continent, were using them for their decorations. Some were using paintings and also sketches. The originality of the Potter is to be observed in their choice and adaptation of these originals.

CHAPTER V

The American Collector

AMERICAN collectors have been particularly interested in the Blue and White wares made by the English potters, especially those which were made for the American market and portrayed American scenes.

Although some of the wares intended for America may have been made earlier than 1820, it is safe to say that the majority were made after this date. The colour of the blue was commonly darker than the Spode blue ; it is often described as a rich dark colour.

Spode did not compete for the American trade ; none of his patterns had American views ; but it is probably safe to say that his success with this particular method of decoration encouraged other potters to follow his example and secure a business in which he was not interested. Moreover the bulk of this American business took place after his death in 1827.

To-day things have changed in America with regard to the Spode wares, and collectors are constantly acquiring specimens both of Spode manufacture and the others of his period, provided they are " marked " with the Potter's name or trade mark.

Very much of our old ware in the Blue and White is travelling across the Atlantic to find new homes amongst

Fig. 3   Original engraving " Chase after a Wolf "

Fig. 4 Spode 10 inch Plate " Death of the Bear "

Fig. 5 Original engraving " Death of the Bear "

Fig. 6 Spode 8½ inch Plate " Common Wolf Trap "

Fig. 7 Original engraving " Common Wolf Trap "

Fig. 8   Spode 7¼ inch Plate " The Hog Deer at bay "

Fig. 9   Original engraving " The Hog Deer at bay "

Fig. 10   Original engraving " Syces or Grooms leading out Horses "
Used by Spode for the 6¾ inch Plate

Fig. 11   Original engraving "Shooting a Leopard in a Tree"
Used by Spode for the 20 inch Dish

Fig. 12   Original engraving "Dooreahs, or Dog Keepers leading out Dogs"   Used by Spode for the 18 inch Dish

Fig. 13 Original engraving "Driving a Bear out of Sugar Canes"
Used by Spode for Dish of about 16 inches and also the Salad Bowl

Fig. 14 Spode Salad Bowl " Driving a Bear out of Sugar Canes "

37

Fig. 15   Spode 14¾ inch Dish " Shooting at the edge of a Jungle "

Fig. 16   Original engraving " Shooting at the edge of a Jungle "

Fig. 17   Spode 10¼ inch Dish " Hunting a Kuttauss or Civet Cat "

Fig. 18   Original engraving " Hunting a Kuttauss or Civet Cat "

people who have a keen appreciation of the antiques of this country.

To such this book, giving exact details of the patterns of Spode, should prove welcome. Though it does not contain similar details of other Blue and White ware, it may perhaps inspire some lover of another potter's work to compile a similar exclusive account and thus to build up a detailed catalogue of a very vast collection of early Blue and White ware.

T. G. Cannon in his book, entitled *Old Spode*, gives a list of prices which have been paid for Spode productions. Under the heading : " Prices of various articles of Spode purchased under the hammer, privately, or of dealers during the years 1902 to 1924," appears the following entry :

"1915. A Spode Ware Dinner Service, with animals and hunting scenes in blue and white, 110 pieces, marked Spode in bluc and impressed mark. Brighton. (Afterwards resold at a large profit for America) .. .. £21"

The service was the Indian Sporting pattern, and although the auction figure was £21 only, I believe it immediately changed hands at £75 ! Today the values of all good specimens of Spode have become greatly enhanced, thus testifying to the great interest now shown in this ware.

D

CHAPTER VI

Collecting Antique Spode

IT cannot be denied that behind most collections of antiques there lies a story of adventure which when told may reveal details that make the collections of interest to many who have never been collectors themselves.

When viewing a Museum one frequently reads the notices " From the collection of . . ." and one wants to know more of that collection and how it came to be formed. How did it arrive in the Museum for the admiration of those who are interested ? Why and how did it come into being, and by what steps did it reach its finished state ?

The beginning of my own collection started in a very simple manner. An advertisement in a local newspaper advertising some furniture for sale prompted me to call at the address to inspect. None of the goods advertised were of interest to me, but I was attracted by a row of blue and white ware which adorned the frieze around the dining-room of the advertiser. Although these were not intended for sale, the gentleman, upon the matter being mentioned, expressed his willingness to part with them.

The price asked seemed to be on the high side, but they were attractive to me, and the deal was completed. They became my property, and, whilst I did not know it at the time, they were the beginning of my collection.

Only one plate, however, has survived this original collection, and it was the one specimen which had a picture and an inscription on the back, " The chase after a wolf." It was marked with the word SPODE.

At that time I had never heard of this name, but because the decoration was unusual and particularly attractive to me, I resolved to find out more about the maker, also to obtain further specimens of his manufactures.

From the various books I consulted about Josiah Spode the potter, I did not find many enlightening details about the things he made. No doubt the inspection of a potter's work is of greater interest than any written word, though the stories of the early struggles of our English potters, their failures and successes, brought back to memory when we view their work, help us to value and appreciate the early pieces produced in the days of experiment when men worked without the knowledge that our contemporary potters have acquired and developed from these early beginnings.

My collection, therefore, started with this one plate, and the resolve to possess others like it.

Alas ! Resolves are easily made but performance frequently falls short of ambition. Although I acquired other specimens, it was eighteen years before a second plate (to make a pair) was discovered with the words on the back " The chase after a wolf."

My collection was begun during the Great War (1914-1918). Because of this upheaval, a holiday which would normally have been spent at the seaside, was turned into a cycling tour of the Midlands, in the course of which I visited Stratford-on-Avon, Warwick Castle (with its wonderful collection of ancient armour and armaments), Kenilworth Castle (made famous by Sir Walter Scott), and other places in these neighbourhoods.

Somewhere in this locality an antique shop was displaying the deep dish illustrated herein of the Blue Italian pattern

(Fig. 71) and although this had been repaired with rivets it was still very attractive, both for its pattern and its unusual shape. I bought it and it thus became the second piece in my collection of Spode Blue and White ware. It was packed and despatched direct to my home, since a cycle was not the vehicle to accommodate such a brittle piece of ware.

My next purchase first revealed itself by its colour. This was the " Lange lijsen " pattern. I noticed a pair of these plates in the window of a well-known London store. Their chief duty seemed to be to lend colour and attractiveness to a fine old oak dresser-sideboard. To a new collector like myself this pattern, being such a contrast to the previous specimens acquired, came as a shock, and for long I considered it to be a Japanese design. It is well, perhaps, to acknowledge one's ignorance !

Many of my adventures in these early days have been forgotten because the addition of specimens, whilst being important and thrilling at the time, came to seem insignificant when compared with later discoveries that I made.

My early ambition to acquire more specimens of the Indian Sporting pattern had not been rewarded with a great measure of success, yet the desire was still present and was satisfied in a curious manner. I was on my way to visit the Annual Antique Dealers' Exhibition held at Grosvenor House, Park Lane, London, and was proceeding by bus along Oxford Street, when my eye was caught by the familiar blue of a pair of plates in the window of a shop the bus was passing. This quick glimpse from the top of the bus was sufficiently arresting to cause me to break my return trip in order to find out more about this " view of blue." The result was more than satis- factory. There reposed two plates (never seen before by me), which were unmistakably a pair of Spode plates of the Indian Sporting pattern, and subsequently identified as " The Common Wolf Trap " picture.

Needless to say, my first action on the following morning was to visit that shop. I examined the plates and found them to be in mint condition and well worthy of possession. I had no hesitation in making them mine. These plates are illustrated herein (Fig. 6). Since then a further pair have been discovered and acquired.

The next most important episode in my hunt for specimens of the Indian Sporting patterns had, at first, nothing whatever to do with the collecting of Spode ware, yet afterwards proved to be an event of major significance. This was a visit to the Spode Works at Stoke-on-Trent in connection with an ordinary business appointment. At this visit I was introduced to Mr. A. Gresham Copeland, a Director of the Spode Works and a decendant of the original William Copeland who was associated with Josiah Spode the First.

The result of this introduction was the link which connected my collection of Spode Blue and White with Mr. Gresham Copeland and his similar collection. The fact that another collector also wishes to secure exactly the same specimens as you do, not only creates competition, but, as I have found, also creates co-operation. I eventually had to thank Mr. Gresham Copeland for presenting me with a pair of the Indian Sporting plates of " The Death of the Bear " pattern.

From this first introduction a correspondence grew up. Many specimens were added to both of our collections, and my hobby and its side issues acquired an enhanced interest.

These side issues, fascinating to me as a collector, arose in a hap-hazard manner. Passing a shop whose business was the selling of old pictures and prints, I was amazed to see a picture in the window which was undoubtedly similar to the pictures which appeared on Spode's Indian Sporting ware.

Suddenly to discover a picture so familiar to me from

my collection was the most startling event that had happened since I first began to acquire Blue and White ware.

Investigation revealed the important truth of the inspiration that had caused Spode to produce his service with the pictures of the Indian Sports. This discovery also revealed the date of the publication of the pictures—1805-1807, and thus gave the clue to the approximate date of the manufacture of Spode's ware. In addition, the stories which were connected with the pictures on the Spode service came to light, and thus these designs became of greater interest because they could be interpreted and fully understood.

Mr. Gresham Copeland and the other Directors of Messrs. W. T. Copeland & Sons, were very interested in this discovery, and their interest was such that they acquired several of the pictures, which they have hung in the Board Room of the Company at Stoke-on-Trent amongst specimens of the ware which were made by Spode from these actual pictures, now secured probably for the second time in the history of the firm, and on view to visitors who go to see one of the oldest of our potteries that are still producing articles from the " Hand of the potter."

CHAPTER VII

The Indian Influence

THE publication by G. Orme of New Bond Street, London, of a story written by Captain Thomas Williamson, who had lived in the East for many years, under the title *Oriental Field Sports, Wild Sports of the East*, commenced on the 4th June, 1805.

This publication was in the form of a monthly issue, each number comprising the printed story and two large aquatint prints, made from the drawings of Samuel Howitt, who was distinguished for his skill in portraying wild animals and hunting scenes. Twenty monthly issues and forty pictures in all were published at a guinea each.

This issue was followed in 1807 by the publication in book form of two volumes of the same story and pictures, but in a considerably reduced size.

Both these issues were republished as second editions in 1819, evidently in view of the great success of both first editions.

The reason for the success of these publications of the story of the hunt in India was due to the scanty knowledge of India among English people at that time, though interest in that mysterious land was stirring and information pertaining to it was eagerly sought.

The manufacture by Spode of a dinner service with illustrations taken from this publication is evidence of his alertness in capitalizing a public demand.

The publications referred to are now, like Spode's ware, antiques and still have a marketable sale. First editions of the large size pictures, bound into one volume, have remained for some years at a value of about £50, and if procurable in their original wrappers, as issued monthly, are worth about double that figure.

The second edition of the large pictures is generally valued at about half the price of the first.

The smaller sized editions, both first and second, are still obtainable, and the prices of these are considerably lower.

Samuel Howitt also executed drawings for *British Field Sports* 1807, and some of those for *Foreign Field Sports* 1807.

These pictures are still of interest and collectors are ready to pay high prices, especially for the British subjects, as the subject of sport was then, and still is, one dear to the British heart.

Many of the aquatints were executed by H. Merke, some by J. Hamble. They were a mixture of line and stipple. The soft ground etching was the work of Thomas Vivares, whose name appears on one engraving only of the series.

It has been stated that this Indian Sporting dinner service was produced for sale in the Indian market, but the writer considers that this is unlikely when viewed in the light of the four different publications of the original engravings which were obviously absorbed principally by the British market.

This Spode Indian Sporting pattern is the most interesting and without doubt one of the finest of his Blue and White productions. A large measure of their success must be credited to the original artist, Samuel Howitt, for producing the original pictures which were used by Spode to illustrate his Dinner Service. This fact alone would not be sufficient to create a success ; the subsequent engravings used for the ware were really excellent, and the blue colour of this service is as attractive as any blue used before or since. In addition to these points, the whiteness of the body and potting were excellent and the glaze like a sheet of soft glass.

The acquisition of a soup plate of this series, twenty years ago, first made me a collector of Spode Blue and White. Although this plate was then over one hundred years old, it was still in mint condition, unscratched and possibly unused !

Another eighteen years passed before I discovered a second plate with the same picture, to complete the pair, although I found a third soon after.

Fig. 1 (Frontispiece) is a photograph of this plate, which bears on the reverse the inscription " Chase after a Wolf." Fig. 3 is from the original engraving.

The story illustrated in the picture is clear in its detail. When wolves venture abroad in the day, it is generally among flocks of sheep or goats, whence they will occasionally seize a lamb or a kid, or perhaps larger prey, and drag it away at a smart pace towards the nearest cover. Sometimes they throw the booty over their shoulders (illustrated in the picture) so as to raise it off the ground ; holding fast with their mouths by the throat, and galloping off fast enough to escape all followers and indeed most dogs, which, though they may possess speed enough to overtake the wolf are, in nine cases out of ten, contented with barking and taking the hint from the wolf's growling, which intimates that he is by no means disposed to relinquish his prize. The dogs generally remain satisfied with a distant view of his teeth and do not put themselves in the way to feel their power.

Fig. 4 is of the 10 inch Meat Plate, also endorsed on the reverse with its title "Death of the Bear." In adapting to ceramic use the engraving (Fig. 5) some parts of the original had to be omitted for lack of space. The original shows two bears, the Spode version only one. The design on the plate fails to illustrate a peculiarity of a hunted bear, which, when closely followed, assumes an erect position. A full grown bear when standing upright may measure about five or even six feet ; he is very broad for his length and his strength is prodigious.

The detail of Spode's portion of the picture is worth a little study. The bear has already received a mortal wound from a spear, also seen. We are told that the dogs do not dare to approach within striking-distance of the bear, rightly fearing his terrible claws, but content themselves with barking. The elephant takes a prominent part in the picture. This fine animal was frequently a member of the hunting-party, and often too, well up in the foreground of the fight. European hunters were always mounted for safety, only the native beaters being on foot.

On the picturesque tree can be observed a hanging pot which tells the observer that under this tree is a live bait used to attract the bears to the spot.

The next illustration (Fig. 6) is of a 8¼ inch Plate, which has the title "Common Wolf Trap." Fig. 7 shows the original engraving. The construction of the trap was exceedingly simple. An old well of sufficient depth was found and a gallows of about eight or nine feet built across its centre. From the middle of this, by means of a small pulley, a bucket or cage was suspended bearing a kid or lamb, so tied that it could not change its position. Over this bait was placed a pot of water, in the bottom of which was a small hole stopped with a rag, rather loosely, so that water might keep dripping slowly upon the kid, which, from its irritation and unusual position, rarely failed to bleat the whole night through. The well was covered with branches and leaves, so that when the wolf made a spring at his prey, he generally ended by falling through the trap into the well.

It needed some pluck for a man to descend into the well to secure the captured wolf, but though needing courage this was not often very dangerous, because in this confined space the wolf usually became cowed and the descending man, by using his wits, could handle him without undue risk.

A still smaller Plate ($7\frac{1}{4}$ inches) is illustrated in Fig. 8 which has the title " The Hog Deer at bay." Fig. 9 reproduces the original engraving. Owing to lack of space Spode's picture does not show a second mounted hunter, considered necessary in this hunt.

In hunting the hog deer, greyhounds are very serviceable because they keep the game up to its utmost speed. The buck is extremely fierce when closely pursued and rarely fails to make an obstinate defence. It has an ugly trick of stopping short until the horse has passed, when the quarry becomes the attacker, and makes a rush at the horse's hind quarters. If there is a following horseman, this stop affords a favourable opportunity for delivering a spear thrust.

A smaller Plate ($6\frac{3}{8}$ inches) was made by Spode (a specimen of which I have still to find) under the title " Syces or grooms leading out horses." Fig. 10 shows the original aquatint. Owing to lack of space only a tiny portion could have been included in Spode's ceramic rendering.

Horses were of great importance, both as beasts of burden and for the transport of man. The use of the horse to aid in the hunt was no less important a function. Much care was exercised in the purchase of suitable mounts with this end in view.

The climate, with its heat and heavy rainy seasons, had to be taken into account in order to preserve the health of the hunters.

The picture shows the grooms leading out the horses for exercise, which was the rule in the morning and evening of each day.

The stable, with its open front, was similar to that used for the dogs.

The row of pots that graced the roofs of these buildings was not for ornament, but for use in case of fire. The roofs, thatched for coolness, were subject to this danger, and the pots, which were filled with water, could be upset by poles or by clods of earth thrown at them so that they tipped the water out and thus helped to extinguish the flames.

A large Dish (20 inches) has the picture " Shooting a Leopard in a Tree." Fig. 11 shows the original engraving, but I have not yet found the dish. The leopard's habit of climbing into trees, especially when pursued, is well known. In most parts of India the leopard is called " tree-tiger " because of this propensity. The picture illustrates a kill that actually took place when the leopard took refuge in a mango tree, after being chased by the wild dogs of the district.

This was an organised hunt as is seen by the presence of the elephants and the well armed hunters.

Another large Dish (18 inches) has the picture " Dooreahs, or dog keepers, leading out dogs." Fig. 12 illustrates the original engraving.

From this picture we can get some idea of the care given to dogs over a hundred years ago, and it may seem remarkable that even in those days the dog was thought to be worthy of the trouble. Owing to the climate, special conditions were necessary to ensure the health of these animals, and the methods of carrying this out may easily be observed by looking at the detailed picture.

The house is planned as a large airy room with the windows facing that side whence the wind commonly blows during the hot season, and a wooden platform round the inside of the room raised about three feet high and covered with mats keeps the dogs off the earthern floor. Windows are not glazed, but protected by frames made of bamboo split into small ribs, intersecting so as to leave spaces a few inches square. Other frames are made larger than the windows and two of them are fixed together with cuss-cuss (the roots of the common jungle grass) in between, and placed a few inches in front of each window. These frames are constantly sprinkled with water. When the hot parching wind blows, it is changed into a cool refreshing breeze which allows the dogs to repose in comfort. We should, in these enlightened days, refer to this method as " air conditioning." These shields are called tatties and are in use for three or four months of each hot season.

During the cold season and rains, the doorways are closed by means of mats fixed between bamboo frames secured at the top to rings fastened in the walls. When they are to be left open the lower ends are propped up by means of bamboo forks.

The dogs—greyhounds, pointers and spaniels—are being led out of their stable for exercise by the native keepers.

The artist has not forgotten the monkey, who is shown with his little kennel at the top of a tall pole.

We have to acknowledge that our grandfathers knew a little about the care and treatment of the domestic animal, and applied their knowledge with a practical and scientific thoroughness.

Another Dish (16 inches) has the picture " Driving a bear

out of Sugar Canes." Fig. 13 illustrates the original engraving. Fig. 14 shows the same picture, on the inside of a deep Salad Bowl.

The bear in the picture is the Bengal bear, which is distinguished by the deep black colour of its hair and by a crescent of white hair, like a gorget, on its breast.

Bears are partial to trees, which they occasionally mount for amusement, or in search of ants, of which they are very fond and find in great numbers in mango and other trees.

Their principal shelter and resort is commonly under steep unfrequented banks where they often take possession of natural cavities or enlarge burrows made by jackals and other animals.

When pursued they proceed open mouthed, with a sharp snarling kind of bark ; this produces an incredible effect on most animals, but especially on horses, which are brought to approach them only with great difficulty, even when in chase. The alarm is doubtless occasioned by the unusual and uncouth appearance of the bear, which waddles in a very ludicrous manner from side to side, very unlike the gait of most quadrupeds. Bears are very fond of ants, for which they will dig to a great depth, tearing up their nests and making cavities sufficient to bury themselves. The several mounds shown in the foreground of the picture represent the hills raised by these curious insects, the termites or white ants, which are perhaps the most destructive of little animals in the whole of creation. They have been known to eat away the bottom of a chest in the course of a single night.

The presence of the bear amongst the sugar canes is revealed by the beaten down appearance and destruction of the canes. The intruder is identified by the marks of his paws which are seen in the soft ground where the little rills of water flow, by which it is conveyed from the wells to the cultivated fields, according to the system of irrigation prevalent in India. The reproduction of this bear is repeated in the border of the series.

A medium size Dish (14¾ inches) has the picture " Shooting at the edge of a Jungle " (Fig. 15) and the whole of the original picture (Fig. 16) has been included in Spode's reproduction.

Here we observe a diversity of sports. Hare coursing occupies the foreground. Bird shooting—partridges, quails, peacocks, etc.—engages the middle distance, and in the background an elephant and a saddled horse suggest that a more ambitious hunt may soon be undertaken.

A small Dish (12 inches) was made by Spode under the title " Hunting a Buffalo." This picture was also used on the cover of the soup tureen, and is mentioned under this reference.

A still smaller Dish (10¼ inches) was also made under the title of " Hunting a Kuttauss or Civet Cat " (Fig. 17).   Fig. 18 shows the original engraving.

The principal devastations of this animal were amongst sheep and pigs. The elephant is seen well in the foreground of this picture, as in many pictures of the hunt, where he seems to have played a very important part in all pursuits of the wild animals of India.

A Soup Tureen, illustrated (Fig. 19 and Fig. 20), provided me with a surprise when I acquired it. Two pictures were used for its adornment—the cover " Hunting an old Buffalo " and the base " The Hog at bay."

Fig. 21 reproduces the original engraving of the Buffalo hunt. Buffaloes were chiefly hunted on elephants, much as tigers were, save that the scene of action usually lay in very heavy grass or in a marsh, to either of which the buffalo instantly resorted when attacked by numbers. When buffaloes charge, they often gore elephants severely, but have not the effect of frightening them to the extent that tigers have. The bulk of the buffalo renders is sufficiently easy to hit, but unless

a vital part is hit, more harm is done than good.   The presence
of many elephants in the hunt gives one the hint that hunting
the buffalo is not to be undertaken lightly owing to his being
extremely fierce, besides being possessed of great strength.

Fig. 22 shows the original engraving entitled " The Hog
at bay."   The term " bringing to bay " implies the resistance
made by the hog to his pursuers, which depends on the dis-
position of the hog, the superior speed of the horses, and the
nearness to cover which the hog will seek if pressed.   When
the hog has been brought to bay, it is necessary that only one
hunter should act at a time, the others holding themselves in
readiness to take advantage of any opportunity which offers
of placing a spear with effect.

Horses often take fright upon close approach to a hog,
especially if they have been wounded in a previous hunt, and
the rider frequently finds he has great difficulty in preventing
his horse suddenly running away from the hog in the critical
moment when the spear is about to be thrown.

A Cover Dish for vegetables is illustrated (Fig. 23 and
Fig. 24) and the picture " Hog hunters meeting by surprise a
Tigress " is also given (Fig. 25).

The picture illustrates clearly the situation that has
arisen when the hog hunters have roused a tigress with her
cubs.   Horses and elephants are extremely alarmed even when
they smell a tiger and never fail to express the most marked
apprehension.   Nothing can force a horse to approach a
living tiger, and all animals that have once witnessed the
spring of a tiger, which is usually accompanied with a most
unpleasant bark or snarl such as freezes the blood of those
around, become peculiarly averse to every object which
reminds them of the occurrence or in the least resembles the
tiger's form and colour.

The picture illustrates an actual scene which took place
when a detachment of soldiers (visible in the background)

Fig. 19   Spode Soup Tureen Cover "Hunting an old Buffalo"

Fig. 20   Spode Soup Tureen (Base) "The Hog at bay"

Fig. 21   Original engraving " Hunting an old Buffalo "

Fig. 22   Original engraving " The Hog at bay "

Fig. 23   Spode Cover Dish " Hog Hunters meeting by surprise a Tigress "

Fig. 24   Spode Cover Dish (Base) " Hog Hunters meeting by surprise a
Tigress "

Fig. 25   Original engraving " Hog Hunters meeting by surprise a Tigress with her Cubs "

Fig. 26   Original engraving " The Dead Hog "

" The Dead Hog "

" The Hog Deer
at Bay "

2 dogs from " Death of the Bear "

Fig. 27   Print from original copperplate used by Spode for Sauce Tureen.
" The Dead Hog " and other pictures

Fig. 28   Original engraving "The Castle of Boudron"
Used by Spode on 18 inch Dish

Fig. 29   Print from surviving portion of original copperplate
Used by Spode on 18 inch Dish.   "The Castle of Boudron."

Fig. 30   Original engraving "Antique fragments at Limisso"

Fig. 31   Spode 16½ inch Dish "Antique fragments at Limisso"

Fig. 32   Original engraving "Principal entrance of the Harbour of Cacamo"

Fig. 33   Spode 14½ inch Dish "Principal entrance of the Harbour of Cacamo"

Fig. 34 Original engraving "City of Corinth"

Fig. 35 Spode 12½ x 10 inch Dish "City of Corinth"

Fig. 36   Spode 13½ x 9½ inch Dish " City of Corinth "

Fig. 37   Original engraving " Ruins of an Ancient Temple near Corinth "

were marching along a road and the wild hog crossed the line.
Several officers quickly snatched spears from their grooms and
dashed after the game. The leading horse was abreast of
the tigress before she revealed her presence by rising and
roaring. He skilfully bore off to the right whilst the second
horseman had a narrow escape, his horse rearing quite erect,
then wheeling round, and finally running off at high speed
in the most ungovernable manner. Although this tigress was
eventually made the subject of an organised attack, the hunters
did not meet with any reward, their horses not being willing
to approach the tigress near enough for the hunters to do it
any damage.

Fig. 26 illustrates the original aquatint entitled " The
dead Hog," but the picture does not fully tell the story of the
hunt. Although horses are in the foreground, it is not revealed
that they arc capable of great speed and also possessed of
considerable courage. Without these two essential qualities
there could be no kill. The picture, does, however, reveal
that the hunt is hot work, as the perspiring hunter is busy
mopping his brow after his strenuous and successful effort in
throwing the fatal spear. The picture shows the spear being
withdrawn, for which great strength is needed, and demonstrates the force which has been employed in dealing this
fatal stroke.

The Native carrying the pole ready with its rope loops for
removing the victim to the camp is well in the foreground
and this is the time when the Syces (or grooms) gather round
to express, with true Eastern fervour, their admiration of the
wonderful skill of their masters in overcoming the wild hog,
which also showed remarkable fearlessness in a deadly attack
on their courageous masters.

In the background, too, may be seen another hog being
pursued by other members of the hunt who have also been
fortunate enough to locate their victim.

F

The heat of the hunters is shared by the horses. At such times particular care must be taken that they do not cool off too suddenly and thus catch a chill, which would, if this care were not exercised, lead to serious illness, frequently with fatal consequences.

This picture was used by Spode to decorate his sauce or gravy Tureen and as this piece has still to be found and added to the writer's collection, a photograph is given of a print from the original copperplate which is still in existence and has been supplied by the courtesy of Messrs. W. T. Copeland & Sons Ltd. (Fig. 27). The picture which was used for the cover of the Tureen is a composite one and the pictures of the Hog Deer and the two dogs were extracted from other pictures of this series.

CHAPTER VIII

The Caramanian Pattern

SHORTLY after the discovery of the Indian Sporting Prints the postman delivered to me a parcel which contained certain specimens produced from old copper-plates still in the possession of the Spode Works, together with a letter from Mr. Gresham Copeland explaining that the enclosed " pulls " were taken from these old copper-plates, and that it was to be presumed they had been used to decorate a dinner service, just as the Indian Sporting pictures had been used.

The prints enclosed were those of the Caramanian pictures, and the request was to find out the origin of the pictures.

They came to me as entirely new pictures, with one exception which was familiar as it was already in my collection of Blue and White in the form of a dinner plate (Fig. 42).

This picture had always aroused a certain curiosity. What country did it represent ? What were the strange buildings ? What story was there behind the picture ?

My first action was to consult the dealer of old prints who had been so helpful with the Indian Sporting pictures, but this gentleman, although very familiar with old engravings,

did not recognise any of the " pulls " from these old copperplates. He gave me the very helpful suggestion that the
British Museum was the place to search for the required
information.

I took his advice and paid a visit to an Official of the
British Museum, who began by consulting a few of the books
at hand, at the same time stating that the pictures undoubtedly
portrayed the sarcophagi of Lycia, the only country where
buildings of this kind were known, and then very courteously
requested the loan of the prints for further investigation.

When I called again on the following day he invited me
into his private room and produced the book containing all
the pictures from which the designs on the Spode ware had
been taken.   (*Mayer's Views in Asia Minor, mainly in Caramania.*)
He also pointed out that certain portions had been extracted
from different engravings and combined to form the composite
pictures used by Spode.

Needless to say, I felt extremely grateful for this help
in locating the book, and thanked the gentleman in the warmest
manner for his valuable help in tracing the book. His reply
was that the labour " was a little fun." This remark on the
part of the Official was to me somewhat enlightening ! Very
little of the serious work of an official's life would come under
the heading of " fun." The request to assist in the tracing
of a book amongst the thousands of books in the Museum,
and the finding thereof (because of his vast knowledge) might
have been regarded as " fun " when compared with the
tracing and labelling of ancient relics two and three thousand
years old, but to me it was an important link in identifying
the Spode Blue and White ware.

The book was eventually purchased—one for Mr. Gresham

Copeland (who was also keenly interested) and another for myself, from which photographs were taken, and appear herein.

It may seem like a fairy-tale when I tell you that about six weeks after this discovery had been made I was in a part of London that I had not previously visited, and was only visiting now in the course of a routine business call, when within a dozen doors of the actual address to be visited, I saw reposing in the window of an antique dealer's premises the major portion of the dinner service with the pictures of the Caramanian scenes.

These plates and dishes, to the number of about fifty, were mostly in excellent condition. I bought them on the spot and they were afterwards distributed among my own collection and that of Mr. Gresham Copeland.

This discovery was a very welcome one, but it was not complete. The soup plates were lacking, also the smaller plates used for pudding or bread, and they are still missing ! Perhaps this is fortunate, because the pleasure of the hunt is still present, and may be continued until the search is finally rewarded and a complete service assembled.

Actually this Spode Caramanian pattern service was provided with its pictures from a book entitled *Views in Egypt, Palestine, and the Ottoman Empire.*

Volume One, *Views in Egypt*, published in 1801 records that the aquatint pictures were " Engraved by and under the direction of Thomas Milton."

Volume Two, is headed *Views in the Ottoman Empire chiefly in Caramania, a part of Asia Minor hitherto unexplored, with some curious selections from the Islands of Rhodes and Cyprus, and the celebrated Cities of Corinth, Carthage and Tripoli, from the original drawings in the possession of Sir R. Ainslie, taken during his embassy to Constantinople by Luigi Mayer.* This was published in 1803, and no mention is made of the name of engraver. It was from this volume that all the pictures used by Spode were taken.

Volume Three, *Views in Palestine*, was published in 1804.

Looking at the various pictures may cause one to wonder why they should be considered suitable for a dinner service. Spode was not alone in using such pictures on dinner ware ; other potters of the time also appealed to public fancy with wares adorned in a similar fashion.

The exact location of Caramania is described as : " Occupying the southern coast of what has been called Asia Minor. Even its name seems little known, as it is commonly confounded with Natolia, or Anadoli, which forms the northern and larger portion."

The location of Cacamo, which is named on several of the pictures, may be searched for in vain on old maps. An official of the British Museum told me that these early chroniclers of travels abroad in the eighteenth century were not careful in their naming of places visited. Perhaps the lack of knowledge of the local language 'may have been the cause of this uncertainty.

From the text of the book, however, we get a little help. " Opposite Castel Rosso is the spacious harbour of Cacamo, or Cacavo, into which flows a small river. About two miles from the mouth of this river . . . are other ruins which clearly indicate some ancient city . . . probably the ancient Myra . . . among the six cities of the first rank in Lycia."

The critic will inform you that, while the places so illustrated reflect a phase of the time, possibly a snobbish phase, when it was fashionable to appear familiar with the places thus portrayed, he and we must regret that Spode did not design a border which was more in keeping with the places illustrated.

It will be observed, too, that the trees which have been introduced into the various pictures are not indigenous to the surroundings.

The explanation is simple when these illustrations are compared with the Indian Sporting pictures. Both the trees and the border have been appropriated from the Indian reproductions to form an all too important part of this Caramanian series.

If on the other hand, the service was intended to appeal to the scholarly, then this limited appeal might account for a select original production and consequently a scarcity of specimens which have survived.

The illustration of the Castle of Boudron was used by Spode on the 18 inch Dish. Fig. 28 shows the original engraving and Fig. 29 a print from the copperplate.

The ancient name for Boudron (modern, Budrum, South-West coast of Caria, Asia Minor) is Halikarnassos, a name made familiar to Englishmen, both by classical literature and the discoveries made at this place in 1856/9 by Charles Newton, of statues, etc., which are now lodged in the British Museum.

The appearance in the picture of a headless man's statue and the sculptures on the walls seem to suggest their being remains of older buildings incorporated in the newer building shown in the picture, in which case they were certainly remains of the famous Mausoleum which was built here.

The present-day description gives the location as to the South of the Gulf of Jassos. The peninsula of Halikarnassos towers like a gigantic fortress. Its extremity is rounded, split by fissures, rendered inaccessible by its sheer cliffs and protected to seaward by dangerous shoals and shallows.

" Boudroum is in the middle of a bay to northward. The town displays its white buildings along the shore, minarets stand out in relief, a mediæval castle stands at the entrance of the natural harbour of ancient Halikarnassos, of which there is nothing visible to awaken memory. In the old days the *quadriga* surmounting the pyramid of the Mausoleum must have been visible from the sea—to-day there is nothing to attract attention."

The Mausoleum referred to is, of course, the famous Mausoleum built by Queen Artemisia to contain the remains of her husband Mausolus.

The building stood half way up the hill in the middle of a spacious square, and was the most amazing sarcophagus of classical antiquity. It has been numbered among the seven wonders of the world.

For many centuries the building was intact; for another long period it remained only partially ruined. At length, however, in the year 1402, the Knights of St. John took possession of Halikarnassos and began to build the castle of St. Peter, from which was derived the Turkish name of Budrum.

For their purpose they used the ruins of the Mausoleum as a quarry for building materials. Parts of the frieze and some of the lions were used to adorn the castle of St. Peter and were thus preserved.

Seventeen slabs of the frieze are now in the British Museum; twelve were removed in 1846 and four more discovered on the site, in 1856/9.

One other slab of this frieze was formerly in the Villa di Negro at Genoa, to which place it was probably transported from Budrum by one of the Knights of St. John, some time in the Fifteenth or early in the Sixteenth Century, and was purchased from the Marchese Serra in 1865. The inclusive length of these slabs is 85 feet 9 inches. Those portions illustrated in the picture are nothing like so long as this measurement, but a careful examination reveals that each section forms a part of the whole; the subject matter is continuous and probably represents the war of the Greeks and Amazons. The Amazons are depicted, some on foot, others on horseback. Their weapons are the battle-axe and the sword.

All the Greeks are on foot ; some of them are represented naked, others wear a tunic reaching to the knees, or a cloak twisted round the arm. Their weapons are the sword and the javelin, together with helmets and round bucklers.

Fig. 30 shows the original engraving of L. Mayer entitled " Antique Fragments at Limisso " and Fig. 31 illustrates the Dish made by Spode (16½ by 12¾ inches). Limisso was a seaport of South Cyprus and one of the important trading ports of the old world.

Spode's rendering of the picture is curious. He cuts off the top section of one pillar to give a better effect to the skyline. Here, too, we observe another departure from usual practice in the repetition of certain elements in the foreground of the picture to make the design fill its allotted space. The probable explanation is that there was a change of shape before a new copperplate could be made. This will be referred to when discussing a later picture.

Fig. 32 shows the original engraving entitled " Principal entrance of the Harbour of Cacamo." Fig. 33 shows the Dish (14½ by 11 inches) made by Spode. The fortified hill was typical of the many coastal ports in the locality, and was a necessity of the times, when raiding was not unusual.

Fig. 34 reproduces the original engraving entitled " City of Corinth " and Fig. 35 and Fig. 36 show two Dishes made by Spode (12½ by 10 inches) (13½ by 9½ inches). The discovery of two different shapes with the same picture can only be explained by an alteration made after the first specimens had been placed upon the market. It seems probable that the oval shape was not popular and was replaced by the square shaped dish. The markings (impressed) are all " Spode," which seems to have been an earlier mark than " SPODE."

This question of marking is not accepted by all, yet dealers in antiques seem to agree that pieces marked " Spode " are earlier than those marked " SPODE " ; moreover, where this type of marking " Spode " is *impressed*, seldom do we find it is twice marked, *i.e.*, impressed in the clay and printed in blue, as is frequently found in " SPODE."

Spode's picture is a composite one, made from four or five engravings of the series. The ruins on the right (Fig. 37) have been superimposed over the Corinth view, and on the engraving bear the title " Ruins of an Ancient Temple near Corinth." The figures in the foreground have been taken from two or three different engravings (Fig. 38).

Corinth, the ancient city, had a natural fortress more than a mile in circuit, and 1,800 feet high. This natural citadel was strengthened by a fort surrounded by the usual wall. The city's strong position, with two seas and the command over a narrow isthmus, was admirably adapted to the needs of commerce.

The ruins are part of a Doric Temple, whose seven pillars still stand to recall the early days of Corinth. Their antiquity is shown by their clumsy strength, and the development from wooden technique is noticeable. The nearness of each column to the next suggests that the builders had not realised the enormous difference between the strength of wood and that of stone. Its date is about 550 B.C.

Fig. 39 shows Spode's Dish, a portion of a supper set (12¾ by 6½ inches). There is no engraving in the series to account for Spode's rendering. I have also an ordinary dish (11¾ by 9 inches) with a similar illustration, but shown in the reverse way.

The writer believes it was designed by the copperplate artist from descriptions in the text, an additional picture being required for this size dish.

Quoting from the work : " Its Citadel, called Acrocorinthus, built on a steep rock overlooking the city, was almost impregnable. On the summit of this rock was likewise a small temple dedicated to Venus ; and just below the summit was the well of Pirene, always full of pellucid water, but never overflowing, and supposed to have a subterranean communication with a spring which ran into the City, and afforded the inhabitants an abundant supply of water. There is still a castle on the site of this citadel, and from it is a beautiful and extensive prospect, including the sea on each side, and the mountains of Helicon and Parnassus, capped with snow, on the north."

Looking at the Spode picture we see a castle, the ruins, a bridge and a river. The mixed assortment of architecture in this picture will lead the observer to the conclusion of the writer, that it was not a credit to the series.

Fig. 40 shows a very small Dish (7¼ by 5½ inches) used as a stand for the Sauce Tureen, with a portion of one of the engravings of the series entitled " Necropolis or Cemetery of Cacamo " (Fig. 41). Although very small, the Spode picture has incorporated the important features of the original engraving.

Fig. 42 illustrates the Meat Plate (10 inch), which was the first of the series to come into the writer's collection. Having no knowledge then of what was represented in the design, I could only chance a guess. The scene seemed to be a cemetery and I fancied that the birds were intended to symbolise the passing of the spirits heavenwards. The architecture of the sarcophagi helped in the later discovery of the engraving entitled " Sarcophagi and Sepulchres at the Head of the Harbour of Cacamo," (Fig. 43) and proved that my guess was near the mark, save that no birds were present, nor picturesque trees. A curious feature is noticeable when one compares the two pictures ; certain constructional details have been added to the sarcophagi,

and these have been taken from another engraving of the
series (Fig. 47).

Visitors to the British Museum, however, will be interested
to see one of these Sarcophagi, which was discovered at
Xanthos by Sir Charles Fellows in 1838, and which bears the
inscription " Tomb of Payava of Lycia, built this Tomb."
This is a very interesting exhibit and the sculptures thereon
are of a war-chariot and the figures of Bear, Boar and Stag.

A later author (Georges Perrot, *History of Art in Phrygia,
Lydia, Caria and Lycia*, 1892) commenting on the Lycian
Sarcophagi, states, " Some two thousand of these sarcophagi,
of which the short side reproduces the front of a house, have
been encountered in Lycia, and in Lycia only. They consist
of a very ponderous movable lid, furnished with saliences
which served as handles and a vat into which were put the
bodies of the family, one after another ; whilst underneath
is often found a kind of vault in which the servitors found
their last rest. These funerary monuments are sometimes
built ; sometimes both vat and base supporting it are cut in
some rocky mass. They were influenced by and derived from
timber constructions."

Fig. 44 shows a tiny Plate (6¼ inch) and the engraving
entitled " Ancient Granary at Cacamo " (Fig. 45). This was
about a mile from the mouth of the river and was built by
the Emperor Hadrian in the year 119 A.D.

The Spode adaptation has been ornamented somewhat
by the addition of a sculptured frieze, taken from buildings
in another picture.

Fig. 46 shows a Dish (8 inches square) impressed-marked
" Spode," probably the stand portion of a Cheese Dish. It is
interesting because the picture is the product of the artist
and not copied from any particular engraving of the series.

The sarcophagi in the centre form the link which connects
this picture with the others ; the three men are figures which

have been copied from one of the engravings, but the other details are original.

It seems curious to have introduced a gateway, walls and buildings that suggest the entrance to some modern cemetery.

Like present-day amateur photographers who are taught to be sure and secure a good foreground for their pictures, the artist of Spode's time must have been guided by the same principle. Thus we find huge flowers frequently presented to the view in disproportion. The whole picture, however, is interesting and in keeping with the others of the series.

Other Spode specimens, not illustrated, include a 8½ inch Plate, on which we find steps leading upward as on the 10 inch Plate, and a very English-looking Castle. A curved section of a copperplate is in existence suitable for printing on the side of a Soup Tureen, the picture being part of the engraving "Colossal Sarcophagus at Castle Rosso."

Fig. 47 shows the original engraving entitled "A Colossal Sarcophagus at Cacamo in Caramania." The grouping of the figures in the foreground is interesting, especially in comparison with a similar group in Wedgwood's Plate of about the same period (Fig. 115). Here is an example of the work of another potter who used a similar type of illustration, fortified hills, buildings, ruins in foreground and a couple of decorative trees. This might almost be labelled another Corinth picture.

Another important picture used by Spode (Fig. 48) was from the engraving of a "Triumphal Arch at Tripoli in Barbary" (Northern Coast of Africa) and this made an excellent view on the two largest sized dishes. Fig. 49 shows Spode's rendering on a dish 16½ by 21½ inches.

A glance at the style of architecture of the arch is sufficient to recognise its Roman origin. It was dedicated, as appears by what remains of the inscription, to Marcus Aurelius

Antoninus, and his colleague in the empire, Lucius Verus, and was erected about the year 166 A.D.

Tripoli, the place name which has been on every tongue because of its capture by the British Army led by Generals Alexander and Montgomery fighting against the German and Italian Armies led by General Rommel, has been the scene of fighting on more than one previous occasion.

At the time of the erection of the Triumphal Arch it was a part of the Roman Empire. During the sixteenth century it came under Turkish rule and was a part of the Ottoman Empire when the engraving was published in 1803, remained so until 1911 when it was again annexed by the Italians.

On maps appearing in our newspapers it is named as " Marcus Aurelius Arch " and the situation thereof on the water front of the Harbour near the extreme edge of the land.

Writing recently from Cairo a newspaper correspondent referring to this arch stated : " An Italian Duce, reigning 100 years after Christ built a triumphal arch as a symbol of the might of Rome. But it has gone the same way as Mussolini's modern monuments. To-day it is half-buried in the earth ; its engraved figure of Victory has almost completely crumbled away ; and its archway is a broken-down curio shop."

The Soup Plate illustration and specimen have still to be located. The search for them is a part of the pleasure and excitement which belongs to the life of a collector. Until discovered the plate is no more than a plate, but when found and acquired it helps to complete a collection and give pleasure to an otherwise incomplete set.

The Dish made by Spode for the 10 inch size is known to portray a part of " The Harbour at Macri " (Makri, Lycia). This piece also I have yet to locate. An old copperplate with this illustration is shown in Fig. 50. Fig. 51 is a reproduction of the original engraving.

Fig. 52 illustrates the original engraving of the Indian Sporting series from which the design of the two cows, seen in the border of this series, was derived.

The picture has the title " A Tiger prowling through a Village." Some of the trees illustrated in this view will also be found added to the " Caramanian " ceramic views.

Fig. 53 shows another engraving of the Indian Sporting series, from which the Elephant and his riders has been extracted for use in the border of this Caramanian service.

CHAPTER IX

The Italian Influence

ANCIENT Roman remains were a subject of much interest in the Regency period, therefore it is not surprising that Spode used the subjects as decorations for his wares. The first piece that I collected was an example of the " Tiber " pattern, and although I had never visited Rome, the design was familiar to me from pictures I had seen elsewhere which were very similar to that upon my plate.

I soon became curious to find the actual pictures which inspired Spode's Italian designs. This picture of Rome was my clue.

There are several print sellers who have large collections of old engravings, for which there seems to be a constant demand, not only among collectors but among writers of books on history, fashion, customs, costumes, architecture, and the progress of manufactures. Even writers of newspaper articles are enquirers for these old prints. I therefore visited some of these dealers and searched through the folders which contained the pictures of Rome.

There were many hundreds of these prints, but my search was presently rewarded with the discovery of a copy of the actual print which was used by Spode. Unfortunately, this print was somewhat discoloured and damaged, and from

Fig. 38   Original engraving of Figures which Spode super-imposed upon
the Dish " The City of Corinth "

Fig. 39   Spode Dish (Portion of Supper Set) 12½ x 6¾ inch Citadel
near Corinth

Fig. 40   Spode 7½ x 5¾ inch Dish " Necropolis or Cemetery of Cacamo "

Fig. 41   Original engraving " Necropolis or Cemetery of Cacamo "

Fig. 42 Spode 10 inch Plate "Sarcophagi and Sepulchres at the head
of the Harbour at Cacamo"

Fig. 43 Original engraving "Sarcophagi and Sepulchres at the head of
the Harbour of Cacamo"

Fig. 44   Spode 6¼ inch Plate "Ancient Granary at Cacamo"

Fig. 45   Original engraving "Ancient Granary at Cacamo"

Fig. 46   Spode 8 inch Dish " Sarcophagi at Cacamo "

Fig. 47   Original engraving " A Colossal Sarcophagus at Cacamo in
Caramania "

Fig. 48   Original engraving "Triumphal Arch at Tripoli in Barbary"
(Northern Coast of Africa)

Fig. 49   Spode 21½ inch Dish "Triumphal Arch at Tripoli in Barbary"

Fig. 50   Print from copperplate used by Spode on 10 inch Dish of
"The Harbour at Macri"

Fig. 51   Original engraving "The Harbour at Macri"

Fig. 52   Original engraving of Indian Sporting series " A Tiger prowling
through a Village " from which the illustration of two cows used on the
border was obtained

Fig. 53   Original engraving " Returning after the hunt of the Wild
Boar " from which the illustration of the Elephant used on the border
was obtained

Fig. 54 Spode 10 inch Plate.   The Tiber pattern.

Fig. 55 Original engraving "The Castle and Bridge of St. Angelo"

Fig. 56   Original engraving "Trajan's Column," Rome

Fig. 57   Spode Mustard Pots "Tiber" pattern

the angle of a collector who was requiring a picture which could be photographed, it was disappointing. In addition, the title was not easily readable. The name of the publisher, also only partly legible, appeared to be " Edwards," with a date in 1798. The illegibility of this imprint made the tracing of a perfect copy of the print more difficult, especially as the name " J. Merigot " which was linked with the title of the book, had been obliterated. This information was only discovered later, after much searching, and after the lapse of a couple of years.

Having only the clue of the date, 1798, I started my search among books published during this year, and eventually the book known as *Merigot's Views of Rome and its Vicinity* came to light. This revealed the actual engraving used by Spode in its entirety. This discovery was vastly important. Not only were the " Tiber " pictures in the book, but also those of the " Lucano," " Tower " and " Castle " patterns.

The publication dates of these engravings were earlier than those of the Indian Sporting and Caramanian engravings used by Spode, and it seemed reasonable to assume that the patterns were the earliest manufactured by him.

Jewitt gives the " Castle " pattern date of manufacture as 1806 ; under the title of " Rome " the date is given as 1811, the " Tower " as 1814, and the " Lucano " as 1819. As all these patterns were derived from the same book of engravings, one would expect to find Spode's dates of manufacture following each other more closely than the dates given by Jewitt. Without other evidence, however, this supposition must remain conjecture.

The engraving which inspired the " Blue Italian " pattern of Spode has not been located in spite of many searches. The actual date of the publication of such an engraving, also the date that Spode first introduced this widely-known and very popular pattern, still remain unknown.

H

Thus my collection is incomplete, and there still remains something to find, which is probably one of the great joys of collecting.

It is well known that during the eighteenth century it became fashionable to take the Grand Tour of the Continent, and to this fact we are indebted for styles in architecture, furniture, books, decorations of many kinds, and also the manufactures of the potters.

One of the well-known Adam brothers, who was one of the serious-minded travellers who went abroad and studied the architecture of Italy and Greece and used the knowledge gained with such effect in his buildings and decorations of London as to create a style of his own.

The result of these travels was the publication of many illustrated books with engravings, which the potters of the time used as patterns to adorn their wares.

Spode made use of J. Merigot's book which was published in 1797-1798, entitled *Views and Ruins in Rome and its Vicinity*. This was a work containing 62 aquatint engravings, which bear different dates of publication and probably were issued in part form and later as a complete volume. These engravings have the imprint, " Published by J. Merigot No. 28 Haymarket and R. Edwards No. 142 New Bond Street, London." In some cases the order of the names is reversed.

The engravings from this work used by Spode were " The Bridge and Castle of St. Angelo " and " Trajan's Column " for the Tiber design ; " The Gate of Sebastian " and " The Bridge Molle " for the Castle pattern ; " The Bridge Lucano " for the pattern of the same title ; and " The Bridge Salaro " for the pattern called Tower.

The " Blue Italian " pattern made by Spode was not taken from Merigot's work.

The Tiber Pattern

Fig. 54 illustrates a Spode Plate, known under this title, and probably referred to by Jewitt as the Rome pattern.

This picture was taken from two aquatints published by J. Merigot and R. Edwards of London, on 28th March, 1798 and 1st May, 1798, and incorporated as one picture by Spode with little alteration. (Fig. 55 and Fig. 56.)

The pattern receives its name from the river shown in the foreground ; the round building on the right is the Castle of St. Angelo, in recent years employed as a papal prison for the living, but designed and erected as a resting place for the dead.

Pope Adrian the sixth caused this mausoleum to be raised in his own name, for his mortal remains therein to be interred. Later it was used as a fortress and the garrison actually hurled down the many beautiful statues and decorations that adorned this ancient monument in their efforts to defend the place and themselves.

One of the curious results of this despoliation was the discovery in the ditches which surrounded the castle of some of these exquisite sculptures and their subsequent recovery.

Underneath the Castle is a series of vaults. Excavations have exposed the ancient door of the Imperial Tomb, besides a winding passage paved with mosaic, communicating with different sepulchral chambers.

Above the huge rotunda of St. Angelo appears a clumsy accumulation of buildings surmounted by a gigantic figure

117

of the archangel sheathing a sword—the work of Wenschefeld, a Flemish artist. This was placed there to appease the wrath of heaven and obtain the arrest of the plague which visited Rome in A.D. 593, and as an emblem of gratitude.

Thus the name was changed from " Mole Hadriano " to that of " Castello di San Angelo."

The Bridge of St. Angelo was built by the Emperor Adrian as an avenue to his mausoleum, but has been re-built and much altered from its original appearance.

The church is, of course, St. Peter's, and the similarity of the view to that of St. Paul's, London, from Blackfriars Bridge, is conspicuous.

In an antique dealer's shop (Rochelle Thomas) the writer found a whole dinner service of this pattern, consisting of upwards of 175 pieces, all in perfect condition, even to the sauce and soup ladles, which are usually the first pieces to be broken.

The illustration (Fig. 57) shows two mustard pots, bearing the " Tiber " pattern and probably very uncommon in view of their extreme liability to break during use. (The dinner service referred to above did not contain these specimens.)

The Rams' Heads in relief at the sides of these pots are also found on the silverware of the same period.

The tall column in Spode's reproduction is Trajan's column, and was superimposed by him.

This monument, the most celebrated and complete of all the relics of antiquity, was erected in the centre of the Forum Trajanum about the beginning of the second century, in honour of the Emperor Trajan and in commemoration of his victories over the Dacians ; it was made to serve as a repository of his ashes.

This column is noted for the excellence of the bas reliefs with which it is adorned. These sculptures represent the first and second expedition of Trajan into Dacia, with his final conquest of Decebalus, the King of that country. The pillar is encircled with two thousand five hundred figures, exclusive of the horses, elephants, arms, machines of war, trophies, etc. These figures, which are admirably executed, are each a foot and a half high.

The column is of white marble of the doric order, and stands on a pedestal richly embellished with superb trophies. Its total height from the summit to the base, including the statue of St. Peter, which has supplanted that of Trajan, is 133 feet. The ascent to the top is made by means of a spiral staircase built in the marble.

Fig. 58 shows a Spode Dish Strainer. The illustration is given because the article is frequently seen in antique shops. All makers seem to have produced these articles which were apparently considered a necessary part of a dinner service. The one illustrated is $10\frac{1}{4}$ by $14\frac{3}{4}$ inches and is made to fit into a large 20 inch Dish. It was probably used for the serving of fish. The provision of this article is another example of the importance attached to the business of feeding in Spode's time.

Fig. 59 shows a Spode Sauce Tureen. The illustration is given for the shape and modelling of this article, which is almost a small size replica of the larger Soup Tureen.

The Castle Pattern

Fig. 60 illustrates a Spode Plate decorated with another composite picture, deriving its inspiration from an aquatint published by J. Merigot on 1st March, 1796. The figure and animals in the foreground were taken from the aquatint entitled " Ponte Molle," published 1st August, 1796.

Fig. 61 is a photograph of the original aquatint which bears the title " The Gate of Sebastian." The ancient name of this gate was Porta Capena, because it led to the town of Capena ; the famous Appian Way passed through it.

The arch which appears in the foreground is the arch of Drusus ; its summit is covered with foliage and the general effect is strikingly picturesque.

Fig. 62 is a photograph of the original aquatint which was published under the title of " Ponte Molle." Paulus Emilius, the censor, built this bridge and called it by his own name. This was later changed to " Milvius." The tower was raised by Belisarius, upon the ruins of the old bridge, and was rebuilt by Pope Nicholas V.

This bridge is famous for the victory which Constantine obtained here over the tyrant Maxentius.

It is interesting to find this pattern illustrated and referred to by E. Morton Nance in his excellent and absorbingly interesting work *Pottery and Porcelain of Swansea and Nantgarw* (1942).

*To follow his references it is necessary to appreciate that the title
" Tower " has been affixed by different people at various times to both
the " Castle " and " Lucano " patterns of Spode.*

In the chapter devoted to The Cambrian Pottery under
T. & J. Bevington & Company (1817-1821) and T. & J.
Bevington (1821-1824) we find the following :—

(Page 129). " The fact that the decoration of the
service is in a transfer pattern (Castled Gatehouse, sometimes termed 'Tower' pattern) usually reserved for
earthenware, would, in spite of the gilded rim, appear
to indicate that the co-partners had decided to treat the
entire lot of the type of china of which the service is
composed as 'inferior china.' The translucency of the
china, which varies according to the thickness of the
individual pieces, usually shows a yellowish-green tint,
but the heavier articles, including the stand (*tureen*)
with the impressed mark (BEVINGTON & CO in small
roman capital letters, and the impressed SWANSEA in
the usual rather large letters) are almost opaque."

(Page 137). " This pattern sometimes called the
'Tower,' is by no means peculiar to Swansea. It is found
on Spode, Clews Warranted Staffordshire and other
makes."

(Page 146) " At the same time it must be pointed
out that some patterns, *e.g.*, the Bridge and Tower (*Spode's
'Lucano'*) and the Castled Gatehouse (*Spode's 'Castle'*)
were certainly copied from those used by Spode and
other Staffordshire manufacturers from which they show
only small differences in detail."

(Page 146, footnote) " In the Tudor period gate-
houses, such as the one seen here, were built with octagonal
turrets—generally in red brick. The pattern is locally
known as 'Castle.' "

(Page 153) " The Castled Gatehouse pattern, a landscape with gateway and two battled towers, which is common to Spode, and other Staffordshire potters."

It was my good fortune to come across a dinner service (unmarked) of Swansea manufacture bearing this " Castle " pattern and I was able to observe the characteristics mentioned in Mr. Nance's book.   The dishes were heavy, the plates deeper than normal, the glaze thin in some places, and on some pieces the blue colour had blistered where it had been heavily applied.   A dish needed to be held up to a strong light before one could be sure that it was translucent.

For those who require a clue which is speedy to observe, Spode's 10 inch plate has *ten* flower blooms (the 8¼ inch plate has *eight* blooms), in the solid background portion at the lower right-hand side of the pictures, in contradistinction to the Swansea plate which has only *seven* blooms.

This pattern was also manufactured by Baker, Bevans & Irwins, some of their specimens are impressed marked in a circle with the full name of the firm, and other specimens have only a marking in blue with the initials " B.B. & I " in addition to the words " Opaque China."

The specimens seen appear to have been made about the year 1830.

The Tower Pattern

Spode used an aquatint engraving published on the 1st February, 1798, under the title " The Bridge of Salaro " for this pattern, which has come to be called " Tower." Fig. 63 illustrates a Sweet Dish made by Spode. Compared with present day requirements, the shape of this dish is elaborately ornamental. Yet these fancy designs were popular, and every maker of the time produced them.

Fig. 64 shows another example of an obsolete shape. The group comprises two knife rests and a strainer. The knife rests, which are decorated with the Tower pattern, appear to have been necessary because the knives were not removed with each course of the dinner, but remained for use with a second or third following service. Some people are of the opinion that these knife rests were also used as asparagus holders when this vegetable was served, but no written record of this fact has come to the writer's notice.

The strainer, included in this illustration, would come under the " Willow " for pattern, but the border has been identified as that which was used on a service manufactured for Queen Charlotte, the pattern being named " Bridge."

The strainer itself would appear to be for the purposes of straining the leaves of the tea when poured from the tea-pot, but, strange as it may seem, an illustration very similar to this one may be seen in Harry Barnard's book, *Wedgwood Ware* (1924), wherein it is described as an " egg poacher."

Fig. 65 is a photograph of the original aquatint which was published under the title of " The Bridge Salaro."

This bridge, built over the Ania, or Teverone, is two miles from the Porta Salara. An inscription informs us that it was destroyed by Totila, and rebuilt by Narses, after his victory over the Goths. It was near this bridge, that Manlius in single combat slew a Gaul of gigantic stature ; and taking from him a golden chain obtained for himself and his family the surname of Torquatus.

Fig. 66 illustrates two ordinary articles, soup and gravy ladles. Their survival is nothing short of remarkable after a hundred years of existence. The writer has searched for specimens of these articles, but these are the only two he has succeeded in finding. The soup ladle has the " Net " pattern and the gravy ladle the " Tower " pattern.

When considering the high quality of Spode's designs, engravings and transfer printing it is not surprising to observe an equally high standard of production. Well known artists, master men in their profession, were engaged by him to produce his wares. One writer has stated that the celebrated artist-engraver Greatbach was responsible for the design and engraving of this " Tower " pattern.

The Lucano Pattern

Fig. 67 illustrates a Spode Soup Tureen Stand which derived its picture from an aquatint engraving published on 1st February, 1798.

Fig. 68 is a photograph from this original aquatint which was published under the title " The Bridge of Lucano." It illustrates a place of historic interest.

This bridge, sixteen miles distant from Rome, derives its name from a victory obtained by the Romans over the Lucanians. It was rebuilt by Tiberius Plautius, who possessed a villa adjoining to it. His magnificent family tomb stood in the same neighbourhood. This ancient tomb, round in form, and much resembling that of Cæcilia Metella, was repaired by the Goths and converted by them into a fortress.

The bridge has become well known from engravings and also from the beautiful picture by G. Poussin in the Doria Palace. It has been crossed by many warriors of the past, heavily-armed against all foes except deadly malaria, which has played a commanding role in the politics of the Eternal City of Rome.

Fig. 69 shows a Spode Sauce Tureen of attractive shape ; this is an exact miniature of the Soup Tureen ; and is an excellent example of Spode's artistic skill in designing.

Fig. 70 is of a Spode Leaf Dish. These leaf dishes were made by many potters and provide another example of the ornate in table appointments. The description of " Sweet

Dish " would appear to be applicable. The reverse is also shown, revealing the veins of the leaf and the marking " SPODE."

The success of Spode with this production is demonstrated by the discovery of another manufacturers' specimen with an exactly similar illustration but marked on the reverse in a scroll, " Bridge of Lucano, Italy." and a wreath with a Crown in the centre. This marking is in blue and quite different to the Copeland & Garrett marks. The colour of this print is distinctly darker than Spode's, but in other respects appears to be an exact replica ; on close examination differences are revealed, clearly proving that a different copperplate had been used in its production.

It corresponds with the illustration in the book of E. Morton Nance (*see notes under* " Castle " *pattern*) who states that the pattern was made at Swansea (but after 1824) by L. W. Dillwyn, and also at Bristol by the Pountney firm.

(Page 147) " The copperplates used for printing such designs (' Castle ' and ' Lucano ') may indeed have been imported from Staffordshire where there were firms of blockmakers who supplied the trade generally."

(Page 153) " A landscape with a round tower, stone bridge, figures, cattle etc., and a border of wheat-ears, vine-leaves, olive-branches and flowers, the same design having been used at Bristol by the Pountney firm."

The Blue Italian Pattern

This pattern of Spode's might almost be described as his masterpiece in the Blue and White series. Perhaps its long continued popularity is to be explained by its satisfying colour, which harmonises well with many furnishings—the oak dresser, the table, whether it be highly polished light or dark oak or the duller surface of old oak. It blends with many coloured tablecloths and looks well on a white cloth. The pattern has the merit of being artistic in all its phases ; a pleasing work of light and shade, with a subject which to say the least is intriguing.

The first issues must have been so well received that production continued during the Copeland & Garrett period (1833-1847) and has since been revived and manufactured in many different shaped articles both useful and ornamental which have resulted in sales of this ware in every part of the civilized world.

This is indeed a testimony of worth which Spode never anticipated when he introduced this pattern to the English market.

The picture of ruins and quiet pastoral scenery was inspired by some Italian artist of the days before the coming of the camera. At first I thought that an engraving was the immediate source of inspiration, but although I have made many searches, they have all been fruitless, and I now tend to the view that some Master Painter first caused this fascinating picture to see the light. The artist G. P. Pannini (1695-1768) was well known for this style of picture.

Four examples of this style of painting may be seen by the traveller in Denmark, on the walls of a state appartment in the Fredensborg Castle, where our own Queen Alexandra used to spend the summer days of her youth. Four large beautiful paintings arrest the eye and remain in the memory for many a day, radiating such charm that a potter of Spode's day would be captivated and wish to immortalise it in his own productions.

In addition to the picture which Spode produced he also designed a border to surround his picture which is not only in keeping with the spirit of the scenery, but which is a continual delight to those who appreciate design and almost certainly appeals to the sensibilities of those who like nice things but do not know why.

Because of its revival, the collector will not wish to assemble many specimens of this pattern. The illustration given (Fig. 71) is an early specimen and interesting because of the attractive deep shape of the dish, a shape which seems to have lost its popularity in these days of small families and small joints.

It is quite possible that the ruined arch, which is a prominent feature in the picture, may be an arch belonging to one of the aquaducts. There were fourteen of these, having an aggregate length of over 359 miles. They were employed to bring pure water to Rome. Of their total extent, 304 miles ran underground and 55 overground, often carried upon arches of great height. When these aquaducts were destroyed, Rome resorted to wells and Tiber water, and the population rapidly decreased.

The tall mediæval fortress tower and the adjoining buildings with their Church-like appearance, in the background of the picture, help to complete the scene of pleasing antiquity.

When considering this Italian picture perhaps some extracts from Miss Dormer Creston's book, entitled *The Regent and his Daughter* (1932) are apposite.

Under the date of June, 1814, she writes :—

"Probably drawings of ruins, for, strange as it may seem after Napoleon had razed half Europe, ruins were, if anything, still more fashionable than they had been in the eighteenth century, and a group of fallen and crumbling masonry in the country of which to make 'a little sketch' held the same charm for the young woman of that day as a golf course in ours."

Writing of the year 1817 she says :—

"It was a time when everyone who could persuade a pencil to do something other than write would do little drawings of their friends, or of ruins, or trees. These they would send to each other to be put into portfolios kept for the purpose, and in letters of the time one comes across this kind of thing written by Lady Eleanor Butler to a friend ; 'Your landscape of Bath is exquisite. You exhibit in it a point of view from which it was never before beheld—your Pen and your Pencil are unique.'"

CHAPTER X

The Chinese Influence

NOT long after I had begun to collect Spode Blue and White ware I had purchased a pair of plates with a distinctly oriental pattern known as " Lange lijsen." The picture was attractive, and, in my ignorance, I thought the style was Japanese. It was not until my collection increased in numbers and different patterns that I made any attempt to consult books, or in any way to gain information with regard to the manufacture of the early ware of our English potters.

To a new collector, like myself, it soon became evident that many specimens had a foreign or oriental appearance, and the association of the Chinese pottery as being the forerunners of my Spode Blue and White did not occur to me until I was suddenly confronted with a similar picture to the " Lange lijsen " pattern of Spode. I saw it on a plate in the shop of a dealer in antique furniture. The sole relief of his display, in a colour sense, was the plate mentioned, together with a blue and white bowl.

The shock I received when viewing this—to me—very familiar picture, was such as to cause me to ask the dealer for particulars. The dealer explained that he had had a

Fig. 58   Spode Dish Strainer " Tiber " pattern

Fig. 59   Spode Sauce Tureen " Tiber " pattern

Fig. 60   Spode 8½ inch Plate " Castle " pattern

Fig. 61   Original engraving " The Gate of Sebastian "

Fig. 62   Original engraving " Ponte Molle "

Fig. 63   Spode Sweetmeat Dish " Tower " pattern

Fig. 64   Spode Knife Rests " Tower " pattern and Strainer " Willow "
pattern

Fig. 65   Original engraving " The Bridge Salaro "

Fig. 66   Spode Soup and Gravy Ladles " Net " and " Tower " patterns

Fig. 67   Spode Soup Tureen Stand "Lucano" pattern

Fig. 68   Original engraving "The Bridge of Lucano"

Fig. 69   Spode Sauce Tureen "Lucano" pattern

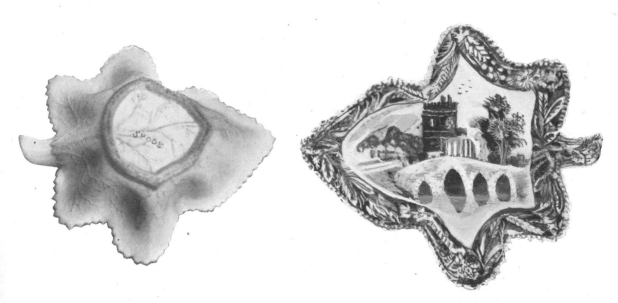

Fig. 70   Spode Leaf Sweetmeat Dish "Lucano" pattern

Fig. 71   Spode (deep) Dish "Blue Italian" pattern

Fig. 72   Spode Cream Jugs " Willow " pattern

Fig. 73   Spode Tea and Coffee Cups with Saucer " Temple " or
" Willow " pattern

Fig. 74   Spode Hot Water Plate " Willow " pattern

Fig. 75   Spode Hot Water Plate " Willow " type pattern

pair but, unfortunately, had broken one, thus he was offering the remaining one at a reduced price. The plate, he said, was of the Ch'ien Lung period—the last period which collectors considered worthy of acquiring, and thus he set about persuading me to buy it.

At first I considered it did not come within the scope of my Spode collection ; it was merely a curiosity because of the similarity of design. I explained this to the dealer. His reply was hardly helpful because he thought that another similar specimen, if at any later time I should think it worthy of possession, would be impossible to find. I am very glad, now that I did purchase this particular plate, because undoubtedly, it was the prototype of Spode's pattern, yet strange to relate the dealer proved to be wrong in his assertion that I would never find a duplicate. My encounter with an original Chinese prototype happened before my discovery of the original engravings which relate to other Spode patterns, and first roused in me the desire to acquire knowledge of the beginnings of the Spode ware.

Mr. Gresham Copeland, upon being shown this Chinese plate, expressed a wish to possess a similar specimen, should one come to light, so that both our collections might be completed. This is where I refuted my friend the dealer, for a few months later I came across a pair of similar plates, and was thus able to part with my single specimen.

Another sidelight on this particular pattern was the discovery, in the British Museum, of a similar plate, or dish, considerable larger in size, which was ascribed to the K'ang Hsi period, not the Ch'ien Lung period, as the dealer had mentioned. This led me to wonder whether the dealer was correct in his information, or whether the British Museum Officials would have a different story to tell me. Upon making further inquiries from a dealer who was an acknowledged authority on Chinese ware, I was told that the period

J

was Ch'ien Lung but the design was known to be a K'ang Hsi pattern which had been reproduced again in this later period.

Some three years later, and in a different locality I made a similar discovery this time in the window of a dealer who specialised entirely in Chinese wares. Quite by chance I noticed a plate (Fig. 82) that bore a strong resemblance to the " India " pattern of Spode (Fig. 81).

I had no hesitation, this time, in interviewing the dealer, and was told that the plate in question was, without doubt, a K'ang Hsi period production—an early piece, too, he asserted. Although the colour of the blue was somewhat lighter in shade than the first Chinese plate that I had acquired, this was no doubt of equal interest in giving another example of Spode's inspiration.

These two examples have convinced me that a British pattern which is obviously of Chinese taste is almost certain to have a Chinese prototype, and may, with confidence, be searched for with a reasonable prospect of being found.

Thus the hobby of collecting can be pursued for many years and give continual pleasure to those who will persist. The interest and excitement of starting out on the search does not diminish with success.

During the eighteenth century there was a craving for everything Chinese—Chinese wallpaper, lacquered beds and other furniture, and also Chinese porcelain—indeed, this craving gave rise to a very beautiful fashion.

It should be remembered that our ancestors of this time were emerging from the pewter and wooden trencher period, and towards the end of the century the tables of the rich were filled with silver, china and good stoneware, much of which had been copied from the Chinese.

Particularly we must observe the china and stoneware. In these days we are inclined to forget that when we refer to

china we include porcelain and earthenware, and class both
as " china." We forget, too, that the name at this period
really meant " from " China, or china-ware, and the present
day use of the word is a development of common usage.

Remember, too, that the Chinese had been manufacturing
porcelain of marvellous beauty for hundreds of years and with
great success. When it was imported into this country, it
became the chief source of inspiration for our own potters
as well as providing patterns for them to copy.

Another curious fact—perhaps this should keep us humble
—is that still to-day very large numbers of our patterns are
pure Chinese in design, and it looks as though they will
continue to be so, largely because the Chinese art was so
excellent.

Not only were the designs of the Chinese copied by the
English potter, but the porcelain or clay was under the eye
for its composition to be examined and subsequently imitated.

Thus English potters had been making porcelain with
varying success for many years, always with the goal before
them of rivalling the Chinese, their acknowledged masters.

It is stated that Spode was the first English potter to
produce an English porcelain or china that was a workable
and practical business manufacturing proposition, and the
fact that his basis is still used in this country by potters is an
enduring proof of the influence of Spode and also of the
Chinese.

As we are concerned only with Spode's Blue and White,
which was chiefly made in earthenware and not porcelain,
we are forced to notice how near he approached the porcelain
body with his earthenware product.

In some cases we find that Spode has produced an almost
exact replica of the original Chinese. We must recognise that
a potter is not always his own master in the selection of design.
He receives orders or requests to produce specific patterns.

This ordering of English-Chinese designs must have caused Spode to reproduce several of the Chinese patterns in order to provide replacements in the services which had originally been imported from China. Moreover there were gaps in the imported ware, which it was desired to fill, and it would be a simpler matter to have the missing pieces made in England than in China. From observation of specimens of the Chinese ware which exist to-day it would appear that the cover-dishes were more common to this country than to China, although the Chinese potter was not behind in copying English specimens, in fact this was done on quite a large scale.

The Willow Pattern

L. Jewitt in his list of Spode patterns, mentions the Dagger-border. This was a variation of the Willow pattern, with the border as named. (See contemporary Blue and White, Fig. 121.)

The Willow pattern was, of course, first made by Thomas Turner at the Caughley Pottery Works in Shropshire from an old Chinese design or designs. The original specimens are said to have been hand painted but in the great majority of known cases the pattern has been transfer printed in blue.

It is safe to say that no other pattern has been copied, by every potter of this country, as much as this one.

It is stated that Thomas Minton, founder of the Minton Pottery, while an apprentice engraver at Caughley, worked on the first copperplates cut for the printing of the Willow pattern. When he left in 1785 he designed slight variations of the original pattern, which he sold to Spode, Wedgwood, Adams, Davenport and others. This may explain why the Willow pattern is found in so many forms.

One writer has stated that " Josiah Spode, the elder, began to make Willow pattern tableware in 1785. His design was very similar to that used on Caughley porcelain but he applied it to earthenware only. Usually these pieces are marked Spode in roughly formed capitals. Josiah Spode, the younger, used the original Caughley design, but impressed his work with a scroll bearing the word Spode, or wrote his name in Old English characters. Willow pattern from the Spode factory is all in a very pale shade of blue, and the engraving is clear and soft. The apple tree bears thirty-two apples."

Other writers have stated that Spode used three different Willow designs.

The actual facts relating to Spode I and Spode II manufacture of the Willow pattern cannot be computed with any final degree of accuracy. This authority seems to have found them all straightforward, but though there may be some truths in his statement, there are also some inaccuracies.

There is no doubt that Spode the elder did make this pattern, and he may have put his mark thereon, but I am unable to confirm this because I have yet to find early specimens of the Willow pattern which can be identified as the manufacture of Spode the elder.

The pieces illustrated in Figs. 72 and 73 are all marked in blue, some " Spode," others " SPODE," and all are porcelain, not earthenware.

Comparing the shapes of the two cream jugs with similar articles of the same period made in silver, one observes a strong resemblance.

It should be noted that other makers' specimens of the tea service illustrated so closely resemble Spode's as to be almost identical. Ridgway is one of these manufacturers, and his mark "R" or a square resembling a Chinese mark, is frequently found.

The pattern " Temple " as mentioned by Jewitt, is illustrated here in the cups and saucers. The " Pale Broseley " pattern was very similar, with variations in the border and in certain other details. The casual eye would class them both as " Willow."

Fig. 74 shows a Spode Willow of the usually accepted pattern, a hot-water plate of 10 inches, made in earthenware of the period 1810-1825.

It is quite reasonable to suppose that this pattern was manufactured in fairly large numbers and also that specimens have survived, but because of the many different makers and the continued manufacture, the original pieces are commonly overlooked and their possessors do not bother to preserve them.

Fig. 75 shows a Spode Hot Water Plate with an illustration which we should describe as a type of " Willow." The specimen is unmarked but is " marked all over."

Although described as a " WILLOW TYPE," the design differs in many details from the true Willow. Even the border which at a first glance resembles the Willow border, is found on examination to be quite a different conception. I have been unable to discover the name of this pattern.

The Lange Lijsen Pattern

We are indebted to the Dutch potters for this name. They were great admirers of the Chinese ware and their admiration took the form of copying the lady of the design and giving her the title "Lange lijsen" (slender damsel). English people frequently refer to these illustrations as "Long Elizas," a corruption of the Dutch name.

The Chinese name was "mei yen," meaning "pretty girls."

A Spode pattern of considerable interest was taken from the Chinese porcelain production virtually in *toto*, with other minor alterations.

In the illustration given (Fig. 76) we show the picture as produced by Spode, while Fig. 77 shows the original Chinese prototype which inspired the design. On comparison it will be noted that Spode did not make an exact copy of the Chinese design. His engraver must have been puzzled by such details as the bridge, which in the original might be a portion of a fence, but in the copy becomes a bridge without doubt. Observe, too, that the Chinese artist has made a bush or tree grow apparently from the unfertile fence top. This evidently scandalized the logical English engraver, who carefully transplanted the vagrant bush to real soil at the edge of the bridge.

The Chinese porcelain plate from which the decorative Spode example was borrowed was sold to the writer and described as belonging to the Ch'ien Lung period (1736-1795).

The resemblance between the two should not permit us to jump to the conclusion that all Chinese ceramic artists were invariably originators. As you probably know, the Chinese potter regarded the duty of copying his ancestor's work almost as a religious obligation. He even included the potter's marks which indicated the original date. An example is shown in the illustration (Fig. 78) of a plate ascribed to the K'ang Hsi period (1662-1722).

The peaceful domestic scene is replaced and warriors in action become the chief decoration. The design of the border, the arrangement of the panels and their intervening fretwork, is very similar in both designs. In either case the border panels show alternating figure and floral motives. The decoration on the reverse of these Chinese plates is also extremely similar and might lead one to the conclusion that both plates belong to the K'ang Hsi period and are original works by different artists. Actually the Ch'ien Lung plates are copies of a K'ang Hsi pattern and an excellent example of the practice of imitating an earlier artist's work.

Whether Spode introduced this pattern to supply replacements to the owners of Chinese ware or whether it was inspired by the popularity of Chinese designs is not recorded, but from the specimens which have survived it would appear that the quantity manufactured was not very large.

The fruit basket illustrated in Fig. 79 is a Spode design of pleasing merit. Similar baskets were made by him in porcelain with rich coloured designs ornamented in resplendent gold.

The illustration of the three-piece vegetable dish, Fig. 80 with provision in the bottom portion for hot water, calls for a little explanation. It should be remembered that Spode had a warehouse in London and that London requirements would influence his designing. We are told that London was growing considerably and new houses were being built.

Those with basement kitchens appealed most to the prospective owner.

Servants were plentiful and wages were low. The basement was the place for the servant, and also for the kitchen —the place for the roasting and boiling. It must have become a constant source of complaint that vegetables had to journey from the basement up a flight of stairs to the dining room on the ground floor and then be served out on plates, that were no longer as hot as they should be, and the vegetables, too, had also cooled in their transit. The hot water vegetable dish must have been evolved to overcome this discomfort.

The middle classes thought much of eating and drinking, and to many it was the only pleasure in life. It is well known that people ate and drank to excess, and one of the reasons for the average shortness of life in the eighteenth and nineteenth centuries was gluttony.

Fig. 80a shows a Spode Salad Bowl. The illustration is included here for the shape and modelling.

Visitors to the British Museum will find a specimen of the Chinese plate (or dish) in a larger size (about 12 inches), bearing a label that dates it from the K'ang Hsi period.

The India Pattern

Fig. 81 shows a Spode 8¼ inch Plate which may be the design referred to in Jewitt's list as being introduced in the year 1815.

This obviously Chinese design bears the title " India " but clearly has nothing to do with the country of that name.

We may assume that the title refers to the East India Company, who were responsible for the importation into England of the Chinese commodities of Porcelain and Tea, thus providing the connection from which the name arises.

It is interesting to recall that at this date the only tea arriving in the British Ports came from China, Indian tea remaining unknown until many years later ; in fact the greater proportion of the tea imported into this country was still Chinese as late as the year 1885.

Tea in Spode's time was an expensive luxury. Evidence of this fact is seen in the mahogany cabinets (with their locks) which were in use at this period. The divisions in these cabinets for the black and green teas, reminds us, too, that the blending of teas was performed by the lady of the house and not by the expert tea-blender, as is the custom now.

It will be seen that Spode's design has eight panels in the border, though another similar design for a smaller plate was made with only five panels.

Fig. 82 shows a Chinese prototype of this design. The border has only six panels although the plate illustrated is very large—about 12 inches. This Chinese plate was made in the K'ang Hsi period (1662-1722). The blue colour is lighter than many for that time.

Despite the similarity of these two patterns it seems likely that not this but another Chinese design was Spode's prototype.

The flowers in the borders are quite different, while the centre illustration bears only a general resemblance by the arrangement of the butterflies and the structure of design.

The Marble or Mosaic Pattern

This was a purely Chinese design, made by Spode in New Stone and later by Copeland & Garrett in ordinary earthenware.

Fig. 83 shows a plate impressed "Spode's New Stone." In comparison with his earthenware it is almost double the weight. The appearance of the back, too, with the footing or ridge, is quite distinct from the earthenware plate of the period, which is perfectly smooth and ridgeless.

Mr. W. B. Honey (*English Pottery and Porcelain, 1933*) states : "A new material of the period was the so-called stone-china, a hard, dense, and heavy glazed earthenware usually of greyish tone. Spode introduced this variety in 1805.

"The characteristic decorations were bastard *famille rose* patterns, mainly in pink, blue, and red in flat washes over printed outlines, simple and unpretentious, but terribly heavy.

"Exact copies of the late Chinese 'export' blue and white were made in Spode's stone-china and some of the dishes in this style glazed over the brownish body are at times hard to distinguish from the actual Chinese.

"A feature of the 1820's was the revived *chinoiserie* of which the Brighton Pavilion decoration of 1815 was an early example."

Without wishing to doubt the information of such an authority as Mr. Honey, I have been unable to discover any specimens of the *Blue and White* on Stone-china made by Spode. Much of the coloured ware, is of course, very familiar. (See under Peacock.)

This New Stone body appears to be very similar to the Stone China, both in weight and hardness, but instead of the greyish tone it was whiter, and more like the earthenware and porcelain (or china) made by Spode.

It will be noticed that where Blue alone was used for decoration or where Blue predominated, the whiter body of the New Stone blended better than the greyish body of the Stone China and may have been introduced for this reason.

161

This New Stone was introduced some time after 1805, when Stone China was first used—hence the name, NEW Stone.

The decoration is familiar to English people from the Chinese " ginger jars " and is known as " hawthorn."

The English name " hawthorn," intended to describe the flower that serves as the motif in this pattern, is altogether misleading.

The flower is neither hawthorn nor blackthorn, but the blossom of the prunus, which is commonly symbolical of spring.

These jars were filled with tea or other fragrant contents and used as New Year gifts. In China the New Year falls as much as two months later than in Europe, about the time when the ice breaks up and the plum-trees begin to bloom. The blossom of the plum, therefore, against a background of breaking ice, signifies the death of winter and the coming of spring, implying the wish that it may come soon. Sometimes the cracks in the ice are replaced by ordinary marbling.

Fig. 84 shows a similar Plate in ordinary earthenware, marked " Copeland & Garrett " (prior to 1847).

The Two Birds Pattern

Fig. 85 illustrates a Saucer made by Spode and marked SPODE. At first sight this appears to be pure Chinese hand-drawn, but on closer examination it is found to be the usual transfer printing.

It is so close to the Chinese in character that it seems reasonable to hope that its prototype will one day come to light in some antique shop. The specimen is the usual deep saucer of the period, five and a half inches in diameter. It is made of earthenware, not china, though it closely resembles that material. The sample is the only specimen of this pattern I have yet seen.

The Hundred Antiques Pattern

Fig. 86 is a photograph of a Spode 10 inch Plate, impressed and blue marked " SPODE," with the additional " A " in blue. A glance suffices to recognise the Chinese origin of the pattern.

Collectors of Chinese pottery describe the illustrated symbols—vases, scrolls, writing equipment, etc., as part of the " hundred antiques," a category which seems to include articles of interest or culture designed for more than simple utility, such as might surround a man of education.

These illustrations are frequently found upon Chinese vases where they are used without any apparent regard for symmetry or ordered design.

The flowers in the border have a resemblance to the Chinese pattern though the border as a whole is uncommon in those Chinese specimens which are offered for sale in this country. It would be very interesting to discover the prototype of this Spode pattern.

In Jewitt's list of patterns there is one entitled " SUN," said to have been first introduced in the year 1822, which may have been this one.

The Net Pattern

Fig. 87 shows a Comport (7½ inches square). This pattern is interesting because, though made by Spode, it was also made by the Herculaneum factory (Liverpool).

In William Turner's work, *Transfer Printing on Enamels, Porcelain and Pottery, 1907*, this pattern is illustrated and ascribed to the Liverpool factory as follows : " Part of a Supper set, old style, deep dark blue underglaze, transfer print, with view of a Chinese scene, pagoda and flowers, diapered in centre." Marked Herculaneum. Size 12 by 5¾ inches.

Turner includes this Herculaneum product in the 18th Century section of his specimens, and gives the date of the Factory as Circa 1796-1841.

The assumption is that the Herculaneum Factory originated the pattern. The facts, however, may be quite different ; it may be that Spode was the originator of this design, which was copied by the other factory.

I have seen only one specimen of this pattern which had the mark " Herculaneum " on the reverse.

As the Comport here illustrated was unmarked I asked the Spode Works for a copy of the original copperplate. Fig. 88 is a reproduction of this copperplate. Careful examination of every detail clearly proves that the two illustrations are identical. The information supplied with this copperplate impression is interesting. " In comparing the details of these patterns which were so extensively engraved (fifty separate copperplates are now in existance) one must not think of them in terms of the mechanically mass-produced article. The plates would, no doubt, be engraved by several different engravers and each man would vary a little the detail of drawing and engraving ; even in one man's work, one would naturally expect to find variation."

Fig. 89 shows a marked Spode 10 inch Plate of the same design, in which such variations can be observed. The positions of the two side pictures have been reversed and the centre ornament is noticeably different. I have examined other specimens and found similar variations.

Another detail to note is the ground work on the copper-plate, which is a series of finely engraved lines. When printed on the body these lines disappear and form a background by spreading, which gives the impression of a flat ground colour. Describing this in technical terms, the original engraving is in the form of a line block, while the printed china becomes a half-tone illustration. The line engraving of backgrounds was only common to the early patterns and soon gave way to stipple.

A further specimen in my possession is marked with small capital letters " SPODE " (impressed) and has the appearance of age, unlike the specimens of Spode II. It seems quite possible that this design was first made by Spode I in the Eighteenth Century along with the " Willow " patterns. It may be that Spode I was its author.

The Nankin Pattern

Fig. 90 shows a Spode plate which may be the pattern which Jewitt mentions as being introduced in the year 1815, under the title of " New Nankin."

The picture and its style suggests that it is a translation from a Chinese prototype without alteration, probably produced by Spode to satisfy his customers who required replacements in their services which had originally come to them from China.

A river scene and in the foreground the figure of a man standing in a boat, which has a canopy and a sail, the man has a pole in his hand and he is in the act of pushing off from the river bank. A little dog may be observed as the only visible passenger.

The Gothic Castle Pattern

Fig. 91 shows a Spode Plate with a pattern that has come in for some very severe criticism from the watchful connoisseur.

The border with its medallions, is very Chinese, but it includes pictures in which appear all manner of animals, representing India with an elephant and other corners of the earth with the giraffe, deer, and a host of indeterminate creatures. A nice Gothic castle comes into the centre of the picture, together with some ruins of uncertain character, a

Fig. 76   Spode 10 inch Plate "Lange Lijsen" pattern

Fig. 77   Chinese Plate "Lange Lijsen" pattern

Fig. 78   Chinese Plate, K'ang Hsi period with similar border to
"Lange Lijsen" pattern

Fig. 79   Spode Fruit Basket "Lange Lijsen" pattern

Fig. 80 Spode Three-piece Vegetable Dish "Lange Lijsen" pattern

Fig. 80a Spode Salad Bowl "Lange Lijsen" pattern

Fig. 81   Spode 8¼ inch Plate " India " pattern

Fig. 82   Chinese Plate K'ang Hsi period, with similar design to Spode's
" India " pattern

Fig. 83   Spode Plate (New Stone) "Marble" or "Mosaic" pattern

Fig. 84   Copeland and Garrett Plate "Marble" or "Mosaic" pattern

Fig. 85   Spode Saucer "Two Birds" pattern

Fig. 86   Spode 10 inch Plate "Hundred Antiques" pattern

Fig. 87   Spode Comport " Net " pattern

Fig. 88   Print from copperplate of centre portion of Spode Comport
" Net " pattern

Fig. 89   Spode 10 inch Plate "Net" pattern

Fig. 90   Spode 10 inch Plate "Nankin" pattern

Fig. 91 Spode 10 inch "Gothic Castle" pattern

Fig. 92 Spode Fruit Basket "Gothic Castle" pattern

Fig. 93   Print from copperplate used by Spode for " Milkmaid " pattern

Fig. 94   Spode Hot Water Plate " Woodman " pattern

bridge, trees and foliage. The addition of a Chinese pot of flowers, rather large and in the foreground, is the most incongruous feature of the whole design.

Since Spode certainly produced this poor pattern, it calls for some explanation. The writer's opinion is that it was designed to succeed the well known Willow pattern and that the artist went astray in his endeavour to produce something original yet oriental in appearance.

Fig. 92 shows the same pattern, unmarked, on a fruit basket with perforated sides. The perforations are repeated on the edges of the stand.

This type of basket is frequently seen with the Willow pattern printed on it. Often it has been poorly moulded, with handles which appear to be stuck on without any care or eye to design.

The moulding and designing of Spode's basket, however, show every sign of good craftsmanship, very superior to many specimens of other makes which come to light when searching for these blue and white antiques.

Perhaps the critics will remember these points with leniency when reviewing this production of Spode.

The Old Peacock Pattern

The illustration in Fig. 108 is taken from an old copper-plate engraving still in the possession of the Spode Works and is included because the " Peacock " pattern appears in Jewitt's list. (See also under Peacock pattern.)

This is another of the patterns after the Chinese taste, and was probably produced in the Blue and White series.

I have yet to discover a specimen of this design.

L

CHAPTER XI

General Designs

THE patterns which come under this heading have been arranged in approximately chronological order of manufacture (taking Jewitt as the authority). The titles themselves to some extent reveal the influence which has inspired their production.

The diversity of these designs is a testimony to Spode's alertness in providing the market either with a topical subject or with a pattern which the lady of the house would consider worthy to grace her table.

The Milkmaid Pattern

Fig. 93 is taken from a print of a copperplate used by Spode under the title of " Milkmaid." This title is mentioned by Jewitt as being introduced in 1814.

This simple domestic picture, if introduced at that date would be the first pattern with an obviously English atmosphere.

I have searched for a specimen of this pattern in vain. Hence I have no alternative but to illustrate the copperplate used by Spode.

The Woodman Pattern

Fig. 94 shows a Spode Hot Water Plate of the Woodman pattern, which according to Jewitt was introduced in the year 1816.

The antique dealer who sold me this specimen made the remark that the design on the right hand handle resembled Bristol ware of the period. This similarity is emphasized by density of colour on this portion, added by brush.

The picture is a composite one taken from engravings of the period, the figure of the woman from a Kaufmann original and the landscape and man's figure is either a Morland or of the Morland school.

The quaintness of the various details in Spode's interpretation are somewhat amusing. The barrel in the picture we must presume to contain something stronger than water —beer or cider—and seems to suggest the thirsty nature of the work of the Woodman; the pointing finger may be to call attention to the work already performed, or to indicate that the lady should depart in order that work may proceed.

The Waterloo Pattern

If specimens of this pattern are in existence they must be of very great interest and worthy of inclusion in any collection or museum, because of the world-wide appeal in everything which pertains to the Battle of Waterloo.

The illustration (Fig. 95) is taken from an old copperplate which bears the marking " Copeland & Garrett " and is probably exactly similar to its predecessor of the Spode make.

Jewitt mentions that the pattern was introduced in 1818, a likely date, considering that the battle of Waterloo was fought in 1815.

It would seem probable that the service contained several different centre pictures illustrating different battles of the Napoleonic period.

The Geranium Pattern

This Spode pattern, supposed to have been introduced in 1820, has an entirely contrasting appearance to all those which preceded it.

The geometrical border deserves high praise for its accuracy of drawing, considering the many possibilities of error.

A striking design illustrating the versatility of Spode's output is illustrated in Fig. 96.

The Warwick Vase Pattern

A " Font " pattern is given in Jewitt's list as being introduced in 1821.

The illustration (Fig. 97) is taken from a copperplate with a " Copeland & Garrett " marking and is presumed to be the " Font " pattern in question, though this is now known only as the " Warwick Vase " pattern.

The scroll border closely resembles the engraving seen on Silverware of this period. As the " Warwick Vase " was a silversmith's product, it is very probable that the design was inspired by a silver specimen of the time.

The Filigree Pattern

Fig. 98 shows a Spode Plate with a design of which the central subject is a basket of flowers.

The general style of the pattern follows the Chinese. We frequently find the Chinese using a basket of flowers as the central motif, but the Chinese basket is very different from Spode's. The division into panels of the rest of the design is also Chinese in character, but the design could never be mistaken for a product of China.

The clear and detailed floral pattern would appeal, no doubt, to the feminine taste in the decoration of a dining table.

Spode was not the only maker of this pattern. The design alone, therefore, is not enough to identify the maker. The marking and other characteristics must also be observed.

The Greek Pattern

Fig. 99 shows a large Dish (14½ inches) made by Spode during the period under review. This again carries a picture that differs in every way from Spode's other designs, and demonstrates his capacity to appreciate and reproduce classical art as successfully as sporting and historical pictures.

A careful inspection of the picture proves it to be a marvellous example of the engraver's art ; the detail of every figure, even to the fingers of the hands, have received minute attention.

Another small dish (a portion of a supper set) (13 by 8¼ inches), illustrated in Fig. 100, emphasises again this scrupulous attention to detail. At the same time the engraver has provided us with a pleasing variety of illustration, there being five distinct pictures ; in the centre and the four corners of the dish, no two of which are alike.

The larger dish is unmarked, the smaller one is marked " Spode " (impressed only) and has in addition a brown colour added to the edge over the glaze. The practice of adding this brown edge to plates and dishes often indicates an early production. Later examples were not usually so ornamented.

This is, no doubt, the pattern " Etruscan " mentioned by Jewitt as being produced by Spode in 1825.

The Persian Pattern

This pattern (Fig. 101) is another of those mentioned by Jewitt, who claims that it was introduced by Spode in the year 1824. We have no proof that the pattern which bears this title to-day is the same one alluded to by Jewitt, but if it is, then it would appear to be the first design to be produced without any centre illustration.

As a contrast to the all-over patterns which preceded it, this design must have initiated a new style of table decoration to a table, with its central expanse of white. Quite possibly it was introduced as a new idea, to vary the many heavily decorated patterns of the previous years.

The Blue Rose Pattern

Fig. 102 shows a Spode Hot Water Plate which is marked on the reverse " Spode's Imperial."

This was a mark introduced by Spode and used on earthenware to indicate the fine body of the ware.

No doubt other patterns were thus marked, but in the Blue and White series it seems possible that " Blue Rose " was the first new pattern to be made after the introduction of the new body, and was marked in this way to draw attention to the quality of the new ware.

The flower picture with the predominating Rose in the border and the collection of old English flowers in the centre, was likely to appeal to the garden-loving lady of those days.

The survival of these Hot Water Plates which may have been for the use of invalids, or perhaps to keep breakfast hot for the late arrival, is not surprising when one remembers that not only were they less constantly in use, but were doubly strong.

The gadroon border, originated by the Silversmith, was copied by the potter and is still being used in silverware and pottery at the present time.

The Union Wreath Pattern

Fig. 103 shows a Spode Jug (China, not Earthenware) of a size suitable for the breakfast table (five inches). The name indicates the character of the pattern.

The English rose predominates, but the Scots' Thistle and the Irish Three-Leaf Shamrock are easily found by the enquiring eye.

The Girl at the Well Pattern

Fig. 104 shows a Spode Soup Plate, printed in a pale blue colour.

The subject is more English than many and the general effect lighter because a wider portion of white surrounds the centre view.

The Country Scene Pattern

Fig. 105 shows a Spode plate and as the correct title is unknown to me I have given it the name of " Country Scene." This name is therefore unauthorised and possibly misleading.

This is a simple picture with cows in the foreground, a house, or it may be a church with a tower, and two trees spreading over the scene. In the distance are more trees and houses and on the horizon mountains form the background.

It would not be surprising to find that the picture was derived from an engraving illustrating some foreign place.

CHAPTER XII

Sidelights on Collecting

IN previous chapters I have given less space to the collecting of Blue and White ware than to the discovery of links which connected the ware with its origins. I have tried to convey something of the interest and excitement which accompanied my investigations.

The discovery of a fresh specimen of Spode manufacture at any time always gave me a thrill, and I carried it home with the tenderest care. As soon as I arrived I washed it carefully and placed it in the most conspicuous position, to be admired there alone until the process was repeated and another specimen reigned in this frontal grand stand.

My friends have asked me, " Where did you find all this china ? " It is strange how one's adventures, exciting as they were, so often seem to have slipped out of one's mind.

There is a simple answer to this question, of course, and that is " in the antique shops." There may have been days in the past when collectors found their treasures on the shelves of village houses, but in these days most of these pieces have found their way to the antique shops, of which there are plenty.

This does not mean that you have only to walk into an antique shop to find what you want. If you visited twenty antique shops in one day you might not find a single piece of Blue and White Spode.

Yet it remains that at least half of my collection has been assembled in the past three or four years, and nearly all of it came from antique shops. The remainder came from fellow collectors, and that has been my only other source.

I have tried to remember where I found my first plate of the Caramanian service (Fig. 42) with its strange design, but my memory has failed me. I do remember, however, how I came to possess the second piece, the Dish referred to after Fig. 39 (not illustrated). How to describe my source in this case is problematical—either it is no antique shop or else it is the biggest antique shop in London ! At the Caledonian Market where you can inspect a wealth of rubbish, mixed with much fine work, the whole being jumbled together with a total disregard for order and display, and lumped into a collection vaster than any I have ever visited elsewhere.

This particular Dish was on a stall which contained mostly silver and plated goods. The dealer did not seem to know much about ceramics, but he did know that the dish was an old Spode dish, therefore an article of value. The price he asked was very reasonable, but in these places one never pays the price asked—it is the accepted thing to do a little bargaining—so after the usual preliminaries the sale was effected and I acquired the dish for my collection. At the time I knew from the impressed marking " Spode " that I had secured an early piece, and when the major portion of a full service came into my possession later, the fact that the dishes were of a different shape confirmed me in this opinion.

I bought my third dish of the Caramanian Service, with the picture of Corinth on it, whilst on holiday, at a dealer's shop in Southport (Lancs.). The shape was *oval*, as illustrated, Fig. 36. At this time I already possessed a specimen of the newer shape with the picture of Corinth, and although the dealer asked a very high price for this dish—stating that dishes of this size were getting more and more scarce and were in good demand—I found it impossible to resist its purchase. I have since been glad that I did not let the opportunity pass.

Although, as I have stated, you might visit many antique shops on one day without finding any specimens, yet they do come to light quite regularly, if searched for with diligence.

I remember chatting to a lady dealer who knew my requirements and she said she had no specimens of Spode to offer. Whilst looking round the shop I spotted the Mosaic Plate (Fig. 83) of which I had only one specimen, and that of Copeland & Garrett manufacture. The lady did not know it was there ! This was certainly one case of searching with diligence !

The other source of supply, my fellow collectors, was the means of my obtaining several specimens.

An article which I had written and which appeared in a magazine brought a letter of appreciation from a collector who lived in a country district in Hampshire. A correspondence began, and I was invited to visit the gentleman and have tea with him. I duly went, and inspected and admired his collection. Tea was offered and partaken of in cups of Rockingham manufacture over one hundred years of age. " Oh yes, we always use these for our tea " was the answer I received to my appreciative comment.

It was with great difficulty that I persuaded the gentleman to sell me the Chinese pattern three piece Cover Dish shown in Fig. 80. He was only induced to do so because he had a duplicate specimen.

From this source I obtained several further specimens. We were both collecting the same articles, and so when unwanted duplicates came into my friend's possession I was able to secure them by correspondence, and add to my collection in a way which would not have been possible had not both of us known exactly what we wanted and how to describe what we had collected.

The majority of my specimens, however, have come from antique shops, and it has been only by paying frequent visits to these places and keeping my eyes well open for the specimens I wanted, that I have been rewarded, in the end, with a comprehensive collection of Blue and White Spode.

Concerning cost, I can state simply that the various specimens illustrated in this book have cost anything from a few shillings to a few pounds, but that does not tell the whole story. It is easy to overlook the cost of the search.

I remember one year, returning from Denmark after an annual holiday, I decided on my arrival at Harwich to visit and spend a day and night at Ipswich, with the sole intention of inspecting the antique shops of that town and obtaining more specimens of Blue and White Spode. I carried out my plan, but found nothing at all.

To which piece in my collection should I attribute the cost of this visit? Obviously to none. In the long run, it is impossible to include the expenses of the search when valuing your collection. They must be written off against the pleasure of collecting.

As a hobby, I have found that specialising in the collecting of Spode ware and the prototypes and engravings which relate thereto, has been a continual source of pleasure and an objective whenever I have visited a fresh neighbourhood. The very many interesting talks I have had with dealers on the subject of antiques in general has been a worthy expenditure of time and money, and one which I have never regretted.

I used to think that Antique collecting, particularly the specialized variety in which I indulged, was inclined to be a narrow and limited pursuit.

My relatives had other ideas. Some of them conceived the collector to be one of those individuals who live in large mansions defended by large walls, and who are served by a large retinue of close attendants.

For such dear friends, with whom we are all blessed, though the blessing may be of uneven character, I have very much pleasure in recording the following facts, for I am not immune to the temptation to " get one back."

I have discovered, quite recently, that the road of the collector of antiques has many turnings. One does not realise this in those early days when collecting is still a more or less superficial hobby.

The collector arrives at his first crossroads when he becomes aware that there is a wealth of other antiques besides those to which he has given his choice, and that these other specimens are also worthy of inspection and veneration.

Many a collector, I fancy, has reached this point and

failed to resist the temptation to divert his attention to this or that object of beauty which has nothing in common, other than age, with the subject of his first choice.

There are many books on collecting whose authors persistently advocate that their readers specialise in their collections.

This advice becomes urgent as the collector's enthusiasm grows and it becomes apparent that a limit must be drawn somewhere or costs will become impossible and the shortage of accommodation will promote a domestic crisis.

I thank those writers whose advice I took to heart when I specialised in Antique Blue and White SPODE ware. If I had not set a limit to my impulses I should never have had room to house what I acquired, nor the money to buy all the lovely things, made in the days gone by, which I would have wished to possess.

When you reach this turning, however, it is well worth going a little way down it, for there is not only much to admire but much to learn.

The next diversion I discovered on my journey was the attraction of ancient cities and towns—for if one collects, the best hunting grounds are the antique habitations.

A good example of what I mean is the City of Chester. The collector arrives with the sole purpose of finding and acquiring specimens. He discovers signs of antiquity in every part of the city, and before long he is aware that all manner of associations are attaching themselves to the memory of what he obtains.

As he walks along the old walls, built by the Romans, which still stand round what was the entire city, his mind, already preoccupied with the beauty of old things, will experience a thrill as great as any that can be inspired by the many monuments of this country. Here is an antique that will never belong to any man's private collection, and one which we hope no improver will remove.

The ancient buildings in the centre of the city ; the famous " Rows " with two separate stories of shops, one on the ground floor and the other on the first floor, remain a marvel of past times that may be remembered, discussed and admired for many a long day.

With its ancient eleventh and twelfth century buildings, Chester is unique perhaps, but there are many other cities, towns and villages that rival its beauties.

Venturing down such a side road as he pursues his quest, the collector of antiques is one of the liveliest appreciators of the beauty of old places.

There is another turning that may tempt him off his way. This is the pleasure of personal contacts. In the course of my travels I have met many dealers in antiques whom I have found to be possessed of a great knowledge of antiques in general, and many, too, who have specialised in some particular line. The information which they readily pass on to prospective customers is usually helpful, always interesting and often entertaining.

I remember visiting a certain city where I had a long conversation with the proprietor of a local antique shop. He told me that his customers, at times, provided him with some problems. One day a lady entered his establishment and enquired if he would purchase some china. She explained that her late husband had been a collector of china for many years, and as he had recently died she wished to dispose of his collection. It appeared that in the lady's eyes her husband's hobby was something of a nuisance, but it had kept him interested and quiet, so on the principle of " letting sleeping dogs lie," she had put up with his mania.

It was arranged that the dealer should call at her house and inspect the china, to see whether he could offer her a figure that would be satisfactory to her.

He called a few days later. Imagine his surprise upon discovering a marvellous collection of Chelsea figures of considerable value.

He accordingly took out his notebook and carefully noted down the necessary details, with the prices he considered he could offer, and then made up his total. When finished he turned to the owner and informed her that he could not offer her more than £500 for the collection. She was agreeably shocked. She had not the slightest idea that this harmless hobby of her husband could be rated at such a figure. Had the dealer been less honest he could have offered her a fifth of this sum, and she would have accepted it without question as fair value.

The matter was settled with an arrangement, at the lady's request, that she should be paid over a period of time in instalments of £50, which suited the dealer well enough, as he did not possess as much money as £500.

With his knowledge of the requirements of his clients, he reckoned that he would be able to dispose at once of some of the specimens which were dropping like ripe fruit into his hands, and he proved to be right. The following day, in fact, he disposed of a single pair of these delicate figures to a collector, for a sum that more than balanced his first instalment of £50.

I have often thought about this conversation with my dealer friend and also of the lady whose late husband's enthusiasm for Chelsea China was one of these tiresome and unintelligible hobbies that a wife tolerates only because it soothes her husband's temper.

Having related this little story I must also tell you about a visit I paid to a small country town in Huntingdonshire. I purchased some old Blue and White in a local antique shop and stayed at an hotel for the night. In the morning I was shown into the breakfast room where to my surprise I found a dresser completely filled with the very articles I had been buying the previous day—Blue and White Hot Water Plates. I asked the maid for particulars of the collection. She replied that it had been the hobby of the late proprietor of the hotel and that his wife would not part with them at any price.

Here was an entirely different attitude of a wife towards her husband's interests.

Another dealer I well remember because he took a delight in adding further adornments to the pieces he sold. It was his custom to make stands and caps in mahogany for any small vases that came into his possession. This was one of his hobbies. He had a small lathe upon which he turned all these articles. Afterwards he stained them darker, polished them and added them to the vases. Being made to fit exactly, and with an eye to style, they produced an effect that was certainly very pleasing.

The most profitable of the many turnings the collector is tempted to take is the road that leads among books. To read works that are related to one's collection is simply a necessity. Many of these inevitably deal with the subject of antiques in general, and with greater knowledge grows up an interest not only in the works which craftsmen of the period produced, but also in the history of the time. So the scope of one's interest widens as the range of books bearing some relation to one's collection is extended.

This broadened outlook is typified to me by a book called *The Great Within*, by Maurice Collis, published in October, 1941, which tells the story of China from the period of the Ming Emperors, through the reigns of the Ch'ing, down to present days.

Here we see clearly how the Chinese export business at Canton began, and how it was carried on in an over-profitable yet short-sighted manner which eventually made competition from the outside world inevitable and lucrative.

The following extract from the book will serve to show how a knowledge of Chinese history can give background interest to a collector of English antiques.

" During the seventeenth and eighteenth centuries great quantities of them (Porcelains of the Ch'ing, Canton lacquer, cabinets, wall-papers, cloisonné and embroideries) were inported into England along with tea and silk.

" They fitted into the Rococo and enhanced the effect of that style, making it more amusing, ingenious, delicate and luxurious. They even harmonized with the music of Mozart.

" The consequence was that polite society became interested in China at the same time as did the man of letters, but for different reasons. Ladies of quality, who might not have read a line of Confucius, were enthusiastic in filling their drawing-rooms with porcelain. As the demand for Chinese decorative objects exceeded the supply, the whole of Europe

proceeded to copy them. German and Dutch glazed wares
were made to resemble Ch'ing porcelains . . . Masters like
Watteau did not think it beneath them to adapt Chinese
designs in their drawings and prints. . . .

"All this and a great deal more—shadow plays, gold-
fish, masques in Chinese costume, gardens, pavilions, tea in
K'ang Hsi cups—had the effect of depicting China as a
delicate, flowery, coloured land, where the upper classes knew
their place, and where there was music and parasols and birds
and chrysanthemums—and Confucius in the background."

In lighter vein are stories like the following, more fanciful
than factual.

A Chinese Potter had been commanded to make a tea-
service for the Emperor. It was to surpass anything previously
made for its perfection and beauty. The clays were mixed,
the various pieces fashioned, the designs were made and the
colours put on—then it was put into the oven for finishing.
The fires were stoked and watched so that the great heat should
be sufficient ; in fact, everything possible was done to produce
a wonderful work of art for the Emperor himself. Alas,
something was missing, the result was not up to expectation.
After the baking and cooling, the service was withdrawn from
the oven and found to be no better than previous efforts !

The service was smashed and another attempt was made,
with the same disappointing result. Many more similar
efforts followed, until at last, in despair, the potter threw
himself into his own furnace and was consumed.

The son found his ashes strewn about the fire, and not
knowing they were his father's, he threw them into his clays,
for his making of pottery. Imagine his delight, when his
work was finished and the results withdrawn from the oven,
to find such perfect and wonderful pieces of porcelain as had
been the aim of the Chinese potters throughout the centuries.
The ashes of the bones of the Chinese potter had made the marvellous body of the new porcelain fit for the Emperor's own use.

Another story which appeared recently in a London
daily newspaper may read like a fairy tale but it was recorded
as a genuine news item.

Fig. 95   Print from one of the copperplates used by Spode to produce
the "Waterloo" pattern

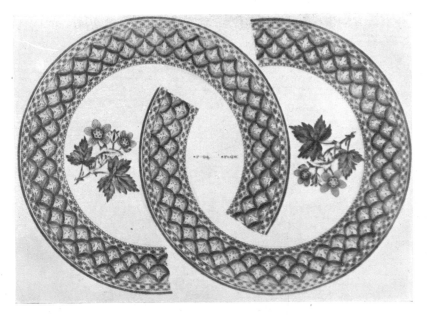

Fig. 96   Print from copperplate used by Spode for the "Geranium"
pattern

Fig. 97   Print from copperplate used by Spode for the "Warwick Vase" pattern

Fig. 98   Spode Soup Plate "Filigree" pattern

Fig. 99   Spode 14½ inch Dish " Greek " pattern

Fig. 100   Spode Dish (Portion of Supper Set) 13 x 8¼ inch " Greek "
pattern

Fig. 101   Print from copperplate used by Spode for "Persian" pattern

Fig. 102   Spode Hot Water Plate "Blue Rose" pattern

Fig. 103   Spode Jug "Union Wreath" pattern

Fig. 104   Spode Soup Plate "Girl at Well" pattern

Fig. 105   Spode 10 inch Plate "Country Scene" pattern

Fig. 106   Spode 10 inch Plate " Peacock " pattern

Fig. 107   Chinese Plate " Peacock " pattern

Fig. 108   Print from copperplate used by Spode for "Old Peacock"
pattern

Fig. 109   Print from copperplate used by Spode for "Ship" pattern
Fig. 110   Print from copperplate used by Spode for "Oriental" pattern

Fig. 111   Print from copperplate used by Spode for " Bird and Flower "
pattern

Fig. 112   Print from copperplate used by Spode for " Bowpot " pattern

Fig. 113   Print from copperplate used by Spode for " Bowpot " pattern

Fig. 114   Print from copperplate used by Spode for " Bude " pattern

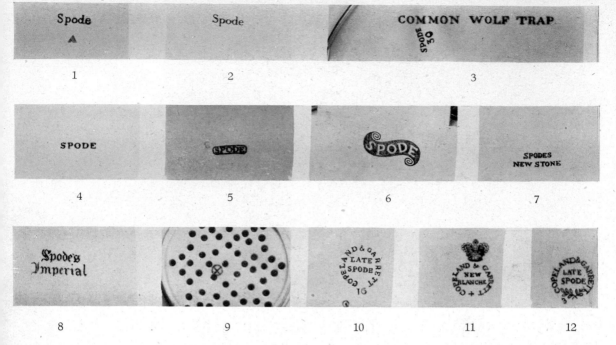

MARKS

1. "Spode," impressed only. This is probably the earliest style of marking.

2. "Spode," in Blue. Used on china concurrently with marking No. 1.

3. "SPODE," impressed, also similar marking in Blue frequently used in addition to impressed mark. ("Common Wolf Trap" illustrates the title marking on Indian Sporting series.)

4. "SPODE," in Blue, used concurrently with mark No. 3.

5. "SPODE" with a border surround, in Blue.

6. "SPODE" in a scroll, in Blue. This mark and mark No. 5 were probably late designs and illustrate evolution of design.

7. "SPODE'S NEW STONE," impressed.

8. "SPODE'S IMPERIAL," used to indicate an improved body of earthenware.

9. Circle with a cross therein. A known cypher used by the Spode Works at the period under review.

10. "COPELAND & GARRETT LATE SPODE," impressed.

11. "COPELAND & GARRETT NEW BLANCHE," surmounted by Crown, in Blue.

12. "COPELAND & GARRETT LATE SPODE," impressed and also in Blue.

Fig. 115 Wedgwood Plate " Absolom's Pillar "

Fig. 116 Supper Set (portion), probably Herculaneum

Fig. 117   Rogers Soup Plate

Fig. 118   Stevenson large Dish with Chinese style decoration

A member of the British aristocracy recently had delivered to him at his town residence a huge crate which, on being opened, was found to contain the most exquisite dinner service. It had come from China, but beyond the name of the consigner's agent, there was nothing to tell why it had come. The pieces were taken out, examined and very cordially admired. Undoubtedly, the service was a most exquisite one. Inquiries were set afoot, and after a long time the explanation duly came to hand. It appears that about a hundred years ago the ancestor of this present member of the aristocracy whilst visiting China, had ordered a service of a particular kind to be made for him. He had ordered it and paid for it in advance, and there the matter stood. No doubt his lordship of that day forgot all about the matter when after a few years the goods were still not delivered. " Those heathen Chinese ! " he might have said.

That, however, was not the end ; it was but the beginning. The order received and paid for, the Chinese potter set to work. To make a perfect service proved to be a long job. The work was started, went on, was handed down from father to son, and because of family troubles remained uncompleted for these many years. At last it was finished and despatched to his lordship as instructed.

And that is why the nobleman of to-day received the crate of table ware.

The story may sound incredible, but it certainly suggests that Chinese potters are nothing if not honest, and nothing if not persevering.

.   .   .   .   .

And so it is that the path of the collector is like a journey, that takes him to many interesting places and rewards him with many treasures.

CHAPTER XIII

Outline Designs

THE list of patterns given by Jewitt was described as " some of Spode's Printed Patterns."

This designation, as interpreted by him, included patterns of the Blue and White and also those of which the outlines were printed and colours later added by hand.

As the Blue and White Spode patterns are the subject matter of this book, it may be helpful to identify as many as possible of these Outline Patterns, with short descriptions, for we must bear in mind that these and many others were being produced at the same time as the Blue and White.

The Peacock Pattern

The pattern known to-day as " Peacock " is the subject of Fig. 106. It is mentioned by Jewitt as being introduced in 1814.

The picture is in the Chinese style, with Peony and Lotus flowers. The plate illustrated is one of the Stone China specimens with the typical grey-blue body which harmonises with its type of picture.

Fig. 119   Staffordshire large Dish

Fig. 120   Staffordshire Plate, probably Lakin

The Peacock pattern comes under the heading of *famille rose*; Fig. 107 shows the original Chinese porcelain plate.

In observing that Spode's design is virtually an exact copy of the Chinese prototype we must bear in mind that the production was a strictly commercial proposition. The imported Chinese wares were not intended for ornament, but for utility. Spode was in competition with this foreign made ware, and if the Chinese article was welcomed in the British market, Spode would have to make something equal or better in order to supplant the foreign goods.

From the housewife's viewpoint Spode's version was better than the Chinese original, whose reddish-brown edges were rough and sharp, in contrast to Spode's copy, which with its rounded edges and smooth surface was cleaner to the touch.

The hardness of the body of the Chinese porcelain, preventing the enamels sinking into the glaze, resulted in a raised and somewhat rough surface. Spode's Stone China and the glaze he used on it produced a body that was not as hard as the Chinese, and did not leave the added enamels so prominent. Thus from a utility standpoint, a better article was provided.

This Stone China of the *famille rose* type became very successful in the Continental market and large quantities were sold in this manner.

It is quite possible that Spode was able to compete in price, but I have not found any facts about prices mentioned by writers on this subject except a comment that the " Indian " porcelain was subject to heavy duties. (Imports of the East India Companies.)

The Chelsea factory also produced close copies of Chinese ware. These became well known and were so successful that they survived to the present time and are still being manufactured without any alteration in design.

N(2)

The Ship Pattern

Jewitt's list mentions a " Ship " pattern, as introduced in 1819.

From the illustration (Fig. 109) it can be clearly seen that this pattern, after the Canton style with the ship riding in the sky, a European port and warehouses or business premises in the centre, an obviously Chinese house and willow tree looming large in the picture, and a honeysuckle, peony and lotus border, needs colour to complete what has remained for the most part an outline design.

The copperplate from which this illustration is taken also bears the SPODE marking. It is curious to observe that T. G. Cannon in his book, *Old Spode*, gives an illustration of a similar plate with these particulars :—

> " A Plate, painted with Chinese figure in colours in panel, with ship in the offing, in gilt surround, in centre of Plate, with the border painted and enamelled with flowers, in famille rose colouring. $9\frac{1}{2}$ inches wide. Marked Spode, Stone China, in fretted square."

This was evidently made from a different copperplate, as the ship is in the centre of the picture and the harbour buildings are different.

The Oriental Pattern

This pattern was introduced in 1820, according to Jewitt.

The illustration (Fig. 110) is taken from an old copperplate, and does not reveal any outstanding merit of design.

The Chinese influence is evident in the Lotus, Prunus, Chrysanthemum and Peony motives. With colour, the whole would make a pleasant picture.

228

The Bird and Flower Pattern

Jewitt mentions a pattern introduced in 1822, which he calls " Bud and Flower."

The print illustrated (Fig. 111) is taken from an old copperplate in the Spode Works and may be the pattern to which Jewitt refers.

Until a specimen can be obtained it is difficult to state with certainty that this is what Jewitt had in mind, or that it was a purely Blue and White production.

The Bow Pot Pattern

Jewitt gives two titles " BONPOT " and " DOUBLE BONPOT " which are considered to be a printer's error, if not a slip of the author's, for " BOW POT."

Through the courtesy of the Spode Works two illustrations are here given (Fig. 112 and Fig. 113) which have been obtained from old copperplates still in their possession. Both designs are outline drawings, intended to be finished with hand colouring.

The central subjects come under the designation of the " Hundred Antiques " referred to under the pattern of this title.

The second illustration has a border of vine tendrils and the first illustration other flowers, not easy to identify, both designs being very Chinese in character.

The Bude Pattern

This illustration (Fig. 114) is taken from a print obtained from an old copperplate still in the possession of the Spode Works and is now known as "Bude," the old name having been lost.

Jewitt gives a pattern name of "Bamboo." It is possible that the "Bude" pattern was the one referred to.

There is no doubt that the design has a strong Chinese influence. The centre picture has a landscape drawn in unmistakably Chinese style, with Bamboos and Flowers (probably Peony), and Birds, one of which at least is portrayed after the familiar Chinese manner.

The border with the sceptre heads, flowers and honeysuckle help to give an Oriental touch to the whole design.

This design was not a true Blue and White as it had the addition of gold, and one touch of salmon pink at the base.

Fig. 121 Mason large Dish of Willow type centre and Dagger border

Fig. 122 Plate 10 inch with classic design and Greek "key" border,
probably Pratt

CHAPTER XIV

Contemporary Blue and White

I N referring to the Contemptory Blue and White ware, an
extract from Mr. W. B. Honey's work, *English Pottery and
Porcelain*, is here quoted :—

" Much of it was anonymous, but rare marked pieces
sometimes enable the specialist student to assign it to such
prolific makers as Turner, Spode, Rogers, Enoch Wood,
William Adams of Greengates (Tunstall), William Adams
of Stoke, A. Stevenson of Cobridge (1810-18), and his
successor, James Clews (1818-30), R. Stevenson and Williams,
also of Cobridge, Shorthose of Hanley (who also made and
marked porcelain about 1800-10), Wedgwood, Davenport and
Stubbs, and the latter's successors, the Mayers, all of Longport,
and J. & W. Ridgway of Cauldon Place and elsewhere, besides
Leeds, Hull, the Don and Bramels potteries at Swinton and
Liverpool (" Herculaneum ") in the North, and Bristol and
Swansea in the West. Some of the printing was in a heavy,
dark, but intense blue newly introduced in this period by
Enoch Wood and quickly taken up by others. The subjects
of the prints were at first mainly Chinese in the Caughley
manner (which originally inspired this Staffordshire work),
and later were typically romantic pastoral landscapes, with
ruins or mansions.

"The starting of the railways provided some subjects, and the great American market for this sort of ware led to the engraving of historic American scenes, including especially, of course, the kind of "view" favoured in the English market.

"Foreign—especially Italian—landscapes were also done, sometimes with the title printed on the back in the foreign language.

"All this underglaze printing of about 1820 to 1850 count as thoroughly original work.

"It represents a new addition to ceramic technique, and has a romantic quality that is often charming."

The illustrations here given of other manufactures of Spode's period have been chosen for their similarity to Spode's work in design, colouring, and style. Some of these might well be mistaken for Spode pieces. This is not surprising, for it is well known that every potter copied his fellow potter. The laws of copyright in those days were unknown, and the only manner in which a craftsman could protect his work from imitation was to adopt so high a standard of manufacture that it became unprofitable for a competitor to attempt to imitate it.

Fig. 115 shows the Wedgwood plate referred to in the section on the "Caramanian" series.

When this plate was examined and compared with the pictures in L. Mayer's Caramanian and Palestine volumes, it was found that the design was derived from several of these engravings.

The most prominent of the buildings depicted is a picture of Absalom's Pillar. The background is undoubtedly the same as Spode's Corinth, the foreground figures and broken stonework are extracted from three different engravings, and the columns of stonework behind the Pillar from still another engraving.

It seems very probable that the engraver who made Spode's copperplates, also made this design for Wedgwood at some later date, after he had left the employment of Spode.

The same picture has been seen upon a smaller plate but whether Wedgwood's service comprised many different pictures, like Spode's, is a question that could best be answered by collectors of old Wedgwood ware.

In the Valley of Jehoshaphat, east of Jerusalem, Palestine, is a sepulchre commonly ascribed to that king, though he, like others is said to have been buried in the City of David. Near it is a monument supposed to be that erected by Absalom in his lifetime, to perpetuate his memory, as he was without a son, whence it is called Absalom's Pillar.

The Wedgwood piece that bears the same design can probably be dated prior to 1820.

Fig. 116 shows a portion of a supper set that appears to have come from the Herculaneum factory. These sets were oval or circular, carried on mahogany trays, and comprised four semi-circular dishes and one central dish, all provided with covers. Some central dishes contained egg cups which are revealed upon removing the cover.

We cannot fail to notice the similarity of this view to certain Spode designs. The buildings, castles and trees all bear a family resemblance. An elephant in the foreground and the Indian type of building suggest a different locality to that which Spode selected.

Fig. 117 shows a piece that is known to be of " Rogers' " manufacture, though it is unmarked.

This pattern is one of Rogers' most attractive designs, but the printing does not come up to the Spode standard. The transfer has been allowed to overrun the edges of the plate and thus detracts from the quality of the production. Without knowing the date of manufacture, I would chance a guess that it was a little later than Spode's productions.

o

A similar illustration, yet differing in many details, is given in E. Morton Nance's book, *The Pottery and Porcelain of Swansea and Nantgarw* (*1942*) with the following particulars.

(Page 137) " The earthenware dinner service, also formerly in the possession of Mr. Gibbins, decorated in blue transfer with an Italianate tower, monopteros, trees and mountain in the background and figures of men and pack-mules in the foreground, is marked BEVINGTON & CO impressed. (c. 1817-1821).

(Page 146) " It is notable that other Swansea designs are similar to those used by Rogers."

Fig. 118 shows a Dish with the impressed mark of its maker " Stevenson." This Chinese picture closely resembles many illustrations which appear on the products of Chinese potters. Yet one would never mistake the production for Chinese. The distinctions are subtle but convincing. This specimen is very similar to Spode's work, and no doubt was manufactured because of the popularity of this style and pattern at that time. It is also a very nicely printed design.

Fig. 119 shows a Dish with a scene bearing some resemblance to Spode's " Gothic Castle " pattern. The maker is that ubiquitous celebrity " Unknown " ; yet it is safe to say that this dish and pattern is of Staffordshire origin, and that the date of manufacture approximates to the date of the Spode ware.

Fig. 120 shows a 10 inch Plate with an illustration of ruins, probably Roman, and very similar to Spode's style of decoration. The border with its pastoral scenery seems to have little in common with the centre picture, except that there is a suggestion of columns, which are neither complete as a building, nor obviously in a ruined condition.

This plate is badly crazed, and somewhat grey in colour (not even approaching white or cream), and the blue colour of the picture has a faded appearance.

The reserve is flat, without raised footing, but has the three stilt marks (the face has these too) which are found in the manufactures of the period, before individual saggers were used in the firing.

It seems probably that the Pyramid in the picture is the Caius Cestius monument, built in Rome about 30 B.C.

In William Turner's work, *Transfer Printing (1907)*, this picture is identified as Hanley (Lakin) and thus described : " Classic ruins and English landscape " Mark—Lakin, impressed. The dish, shell pattern, is stated to be in the Victoria and Albert Museum, South Kensington. The date of manufacture is given as the late eighteenth and early nineteenth centuries.

Fig. 121 is the " Dagger Border " referred to in Jewitt's list. Although the centre design is described as a " Willow " type, there is considerable variation from that design. This border is still reproduced on modern ware, sometimes on cups and saucers, and in a more subdued colour and form. The Dish here illustrated was made by Mason ; it has a coat of arms and " Impd. Iron Stone China, Stoke Works," in blue on the reverse.

Fig. 122 is an illustration of a Plate with classic design and Greek " Key " border, similar to the Spode Greek pattern illustrated in this book. It will be observed that Spode's designs have central patterns of Greek figures, whilst the plate here illustrated has a floral centre.

The two patterns are very similar in style and it is not surprising to find that N. Hudson Moore illustrating this plate in his book, *The Old China Book* (published in New York in 1903) ascribes it to Spode.

The specimen from which this photograph was taken does not give any maker's name or other identification marks (possibly Pratt of Fenton). It is certainly of about the same period as Spode, and has the brown edge found on early Blue and White ware, but it has no other detail other than similarity of pattern to suggest that Spode made it.

Not long ago I saw yet another variation of this Classic design, on a product of some other unknown maker ; it was octagonal in shape and had much the same general appearance as Spode's pieces and the plate illustrated here. The figures are in the style of Flaxman.

CHAPTER XV

Royal Recognition of Spode's work

THE Prince of Wales (Regent 1811-1820, reigning as George IV, 1820-1830) with his brother, the Duke of Clarence, made a visit to the Spode Works in 1806 and was greatly interested in all he saw there, particularly in the Felspar Porcelain which was then one of Spode's newest products.

As a result of this visit Josiah Spode II was appointed " Potter to His Royal Highness the Prince of Wales."

A service was made for the Prince and was marked with the Prince of Wales' feathers in token of this appointment.

The mother of the Prince (Queen Charlotte) also visited the Works on the 3rd July, 1817, accompanied by the Princess Elizabeth, and ordered different wares, including an Iron Stone Dinner Service, of which pieces still survive.

The Duke of Kent (fourth son of George III and father of Queen Victoria) was a purchaser of a Dinner Service which eventually became the property of and was frequently used by Queen Victoria.

A Service of historic interest was one made and marked " Used at the Coronation of His Majesty George IV, 19th July, 1821."

239

INDEX

Index

Index